Compound interest is the "Eighth Wonder of the World," and Ed explains its power in a way that is clear and meaningful to students and young adults.
—William Selby, Managing Director, Gabelli Asset Management Investment Management Firm

I have used Ed's concepts to start a fund for my newborn grandchild. I believe the $2,000 gift I have given her can accumulate to more than $1,000,000 by the time she is in middle age.
—Dr. Robert Foster, President Emeritus, Northwest Missouri State University

. . . My college students learned a great deal from Ed's concepts. I think a number of them will think very seriously about starting a savings and investing program. He stressed it is the discipline and the regularity, not the amount, that counts. I only wish I had done this when I was younger.
—Gloria Gabel, University of Missouri Kansas City

The Jump$tart Coalition for Personal Financial Literacy believes in the importance of teaching our youth personal finance instruction. Ed's book can help students understand the importance of saving and the difference that it can make in their lives. He covers many other important financial concepts including investments, safety and diversification, tax shelters, Roth IRAs, 529 Plans, etc.

—DARA DUGUAY, EXECUTIVE DIRECTOR, JUMP$TART COALITION

Ed spoke to my entire student body and my teaching faculty about making $1,000,000 with only $2,000. His explanation of the Rule of 72 was eye opening to our students. I believe this can benefit every student and young person.

—DOUGLAS R. HENRY, PRINCIPAL, BROOKFIELD HIGH SCHOOL

Ed has done a wonderful job explaining some basic and important financial concepts to young people. We've used some of his materials on our Web site at www.aba.com and we feel that parents and grandparents would find his book to be a valuable resource.

—SUSAN COLE, DIRECTOR, AMERICAN BANKERS ASSOCIATION EDUCATION FOUNDATION

Ed appeared as a panelist on our PBS television show entitled "Making Your Kid a Millionaire." His passionate ideas on the importance of saving early in life are clear and concise and, if implemented, will enhance the financial prospects for today's youth by 1,000%.

—DENNIS MCCUISTION, HOST, *MCCUISTION* ON PBS

The principle of compounding is one of the most undervalued concepts by the general public. The sad thing is that if we understood it better, retirement would not become the financial burden that weighs on our mind. Using the principles in this book is the answer to a comfortable retirement.

—SUZANNE SHORT, AUTHOR, *WISDOM DADDY TAUGHT ME: A PATH FROM POVERTY TO PROSPERITY*

MAKING A MILLION WITH ONLY $2,000

MAKING A MILLION
WITH ONLY $2,000

EVERY YOUNG PERSON CAN DO IT

ED DOUGLAS

BROWN BOOKS PUBLISHING GROUP
DALLAS

For information, please contact Brown Books Publishing Group
16200 North Dallas Parkway, Suite 225, Dallas, Texas 75248
972-381-0009   www.brownbooks.com

First Printing, 2002
ISBN 0-9722681-0-3
LCCN 2002093257

Printed and bound in the United States of America

READERS OF THIS BOOK SHOULD BEAR IN MIND THE FOLLOWING:
This book is written to provide the reader with general information concerning personal investing for the long term. It does not address specific investment objectives, financial situations or particular needs of any investor. Each investor should seek advice from his/her own professional advisors. Some of the materials in this book have been obtained from resources which are believed to be reliable, but the accuracy or completeness of such information cannot be guaranteed. Past investment performance is no assurance as to future investment performance. An investor in stocks, mutual funds, and other securities may receive less than originally invested. Furthermore, stocks and mutual fund securities are not insured or guaranteed by the government, the FDIC, or any other agency of the government.

DEDICATION

This book is dedicated to my family: my wife, Marla, and our three children, Jared, Aaron, and Kaylee. They have made my life very special with their love and support. Also thanks to my mom and dad, for their upbringing, and my older brother, Richard. The three of them gave me direction and lived good examples, setting me on the right course early in my life.

C ONTENTS

Dedication   vii

Contents   ix

Purpose   xi

Preface   xiii

Acknowledgments   xv

I   In the Beginning
The Gift   1

II   What Is Wealthy?
How Much Is a Million Dollars Worth?   9

III   Factors That Make Compounding Work   19

IV   The Rule of 72   31

V   The Investment of Choice   37

VI	The Effect of Taxes and How to Minimize Their Effect	57
VII	Safety, Diversification	67
VIII	Keeping Costs Down and Index Funds	75
IX	Spending Less Than You Earn	85
X	The Roth Individual Retirement Account	97
XI	Strategies	109
XII	Additional Strategies (for Parents and Grandparents)	115
XIII	When Do I Enjoy It?	125
XIV	What Can Go Wrong?	133
XV	I Don't Have $2,000!	139
XVI	What Have We Learned?	145
	About the Author	153

PURPOSE

THIS book is written to help young adults ages fifteen to thirty-five and parents and grandparents of children in that age range. Its purpose is to teach young adults the importance and value of saving money early in life. Alternately, this book shows parents and grandparents how they can make a small gift to their children that could someday be worth a million dollars or more. It explains in detail the power of growth and interest and its component parts: time, return, and compounding. It explains the Rule of 72, which shows how quickly money can double using a given interest rate. Further, it shows how to maximize investment returns safely for the long-term and how to minimize and shelter taxes while minimizing costs. Finally, the book shows how anyone can realistically grow $2,000 into $1,000,000.

This book is not a get-rich-quick scheme. It is about a disciplined approach to long-term accumulation of wealth. Note to parents and grandparents: the application of these methods can potentially make a huge difference in your children's financial future and can, therefore, be the most important educational gift you can give them.

PREFACE

A PERFECT TIME TO INVEST FOR THE LONG RUN

AS we went to press shortly after July 31, 2002, the stock market as measured by the S & P 500 was down -19.9% for the year. One of the reasons for this decline was concern about corporate misrepresentations and scandals of companies such as Enron, Tyco, Adelphia and WorldCom. This follows successive down years by the S & P 500, down -9.08% for calendar year 2000 and down -11.88% for calendar year 2001. If 2002 finishes down, it will be the first three successive down years since 1939-1941.

This pessimism has and will drive many investors away from stock investments for some period of time until their confidence is restored.

Based on the above, it might seem that this is the wrong time to invest for the long haul. Actually, I believe the reverse is true. For long-term investors, this is a perfect time to make a one-time investment or to begin an investment program.

Historically, markets move to extremes either way as investor optimism becomes overly bullish or, in this case, as investor pessimism becomes overly bearish. After moving to extremes, there is always a reversion to the mean or a moving back to historic returns.

Based on $2\frac{1}{2}$ years of a market decline, I believe that a reversion to historical returns will happen in the next few months or next few years. Either way, this is an excellent time to begin the discipline of saving and investing regularly when many others have lost confidence. Follow the principles in this book and be patient. I am confident American ingenuity and the strength of our capitalist system can potentially make $2,000 grow to $1,000,000.

ACKNOWLEDGMENTS

I would like to thank the Board of Directors of the Citizens Bancshares Company of Chillicothe, Missouri for their understanding and encouragement in my efforts to promote this book's message to students and young adults. Without their support this would not have been possible.

Small Investments can turn into a pot of gold!

I

In the Beginning
The Gift

LET'S start this book with a guessing game. Imagine that when you were ten years old your grandmother gave you $2,000 of XYZ Company stock. She asked that it not be sold until you were much older, so your dad put it in his lockbox at the bank. You forgot about it until your dad died at age 88, when you found the stock certificate.

You are now 65; it has been 55 years since your grandmother gave you the gift. Not knowing what XYZ stock is worth, you call a broker friend. He researches the stock and reports that during the last 55 years it has grown at a rate of return that is average for the overall stock market.

Your comment to your broker friend is, "Okay, so it has performed average. What is it worth now?"

Your broker friend likes to play games, and he says to you, "Why don't you guess what it's worth?"

Before you read further, make sure you guess.

Remember that it was worth $2,000 when it was given to you, and it has been a long time—but he has told you it has performed only "average."

So you say, "$20,000."

He says, "No, it is much higher."

You guess $50,000.

"You are still very low."

You guess $100,000.

"It is still too low."

"I am sick of this guessing game. Tell me what it is worth!"

He tells you to sit down. "It is worth $1,018,641.21!"

You think your broker has lost his mind, but he explains to you that he has double-checked his figures, and he is quite sure he is accurate.

This story is, in fact, very possible.[1] The stock market has compounded at an average return of approximately

---

[1] If the stock in this example paid dividends, you would have remembered you owned it because of the quarterly dividends you would have received. However, some stocks pay very little or no dividends, as is assumed to be the case in our example. Some companies pay stock dividends, in which case new shares are issued, but even then there is no tax effect and you still might not know what the overall value is without further research. It is also possible that your grandmother could have put the stock in her son's (your dad's) name as custodian and used her address or your dad's address for information from the company such as annual reports, in which case you again may be unlikely to be aware of your ownership.

12%[2] annually since 1926. The past is most likely the best estimate of the future or of what will happen in the next 55 years. Two thousand dollars grew to over $1,000,000 with time and an average stock market compounded rate of return. It is that simple. If an individual lets time, a reasonable investment return, and compounding of money work for him or her, almost any young person could be a millionaire—or multimillionaire—at some point.

Although my personal experience is not exactly as the story just described, there are a few similarities. When I was in my early teens, my dad gave me a few shares of stock of a small bank where he and my grandfather had served as bank directors. Eight or ten years later, this bank was sold and I received $2,200. My mother and my maternal grandfather had always told me, "Save your money." My

---

DEFINING SOME BASIC TERMS

An **INVESTMENT** is the investing of money or capital to gain interest or income.

A **STOCK** is the capital raised by a corporation through the sale of shares that entitle the holder to interest or dividends and to part ownership into the company.

INTEREST is payment for the use of money or credit, usually expressed as a percentage of the amount owed or used.

---

[2] The geometric mean or compounded annual return for large capitalization stocks from 1926 through 2001 is 10.7%. The arithmetic mean or average annual return for large capitalization stocks from 1926 through 2001 is 12.8%. The geometric or compounded annual return for small capitalization stocks from 1926 through 2001 is 12.5%, while the average annual return is 17.4%. Using an average geometric or compounded return for large and small stocks together approximates 12% (10.7% + 12.5% ÷ 2 = 11.6%). When the first edition of this book was written in December 2000, the average compounded return was 12%, but including two years of lower stock prices in 2000 and 2001 lowers the return slightly to 11.6%, which still approximates 12%. This information comes from Merrill Lynch Consulting using Ibbotson Data.

grandfather had made it through the depression, and he permanently imparted this idea to my mom, and then it was subsequently drilled into me from both of them. Consequently, the bank stock proceeds, along with other money I saved, was first put in bank certificates of deposit and then, a few years later, into stock funds that, over time, did very, very well. The fictional story and my story are not unique. Many others who follow the discipline of saving early and regularly in life and who also combine it with prudent investment choices have had similar results. What follows in this book will show how you, too, can save and invest wisely to reach sizeable wealth.

Why do stocks go up? The full explanation of this is beyond the scope of this book. Generally, though, stocks can go up or down based on the profits a company earns, the dividends the company pays to shareholders, and people's expectations for future earnings and dividends. Over time, overall stock market prices rise for a number of reasons. First, the gross domestic profit of the economy tends to grow at about 6% per year, which is a combination of inflation and improved productivity. The growth in population is one factor that creates additional demand for products. Productivity increases with more advanced technology, like computers and other machines, and improved methods of sales and production. Company profits, and therefore stock prices, grow with the economy, plus the shareholder receives an additional return of cash dividends or, more recently, company stock buybacks that benefit the shareholder like a dividend. As long as our free enterprise system encourages people to profit from new and innovative products and services, stocks will tend to rise.

THE IMPORTANCE OF TIME

The combination of interest and investment returns and time allowed to compound are very powerful tools. You may remember the story of the Native Americans who sold the island of Manhattan in 1626 for $24 in beads and trinkets.

Some people tell this story implying that the Native Americans made a terrible deal selling Manhattan for such a low price. However, if you would assume they took the $24 and invested it at a 6% compounded rate of return, it would now be worth $74,157,900,000 (almost $75 billion in 375 years). Maybe the Native

> Native Americans sold Manhattan for $24 in trinkets in 1626. At a 6% compounded rate of return, that $24 is now worth how much?
>
> Answer:
> $74,157,900,000—
> almost $75 billion

Americans didn't get such a bad deal after all? However, we don't know what they actually did with the trinkets.

THE IMPORTANCE OF A HIGH COMPOUND RETURN

It was in October 1999 that the world reached six billion in population, or 6,000,000,000 people. Let's say that we are charitably inclined and want to give every person in the world a million dollars ($1,000,000). That would require 6,000,000,000 x $1,000,000 = $6,000,000,000,000,000, or six thousand trillion dollars. If you could save $2,000 once in a Roth IRA (more on this in a later chapter) and have it grow at 12% tax-free forever (average stock return in a Roth IRA), how long would it take to accumulate six thousand trillion, or enough to give every man, woman, and child in the world one million dollars?

At the end of 100 years, you will have accumulated $167,044,531 ($167 million). At 150 years, you will have accumulated $2,839,767,793 (almost $3 billion). At 200 years, you will have accumulated $13,951,940,000,000, almost $14 thousand billion. At 250 years, you will have grown to $4,032,141,000,000,000, or over $4 thousand trillion. Somewhere in the 254th year, you would pass the six thousand trillion dollar mark, allowing you to give every person on earth one million dollars.[3]

> Six billion people in the world multiplied by $1 million per person = $6 thousand trillion
>
> How long would it take $2,000 growing at 12% to equal $6 thousand trillion?
>
> Answer: 254 years

Does this show you the power of compounding? In practice, this has not happened for several reasons. For one, 12% stock returns have been recorded accurately going back to 1926, only 75 years through 2001. It should be noted that this return includes the down periods of the stock market including, among others, the Great Depression years of the early '30s, the bear market of 1973–1974, the market crash of 1987, and the first two plus years of the bear market that began in 2000. Second, money is normally spent, given away, or left as an inheritance and then spent or frittered away by successive generations. Finally, income and capital gains taxes and estate taxes normally cut into wealth substantially (50% estate tax rate on large estates for 2002). With the Roth IRA (tax-free growth), wise investments, increasingly longer lives due to advances in modern medicine, and a strong char-

[3] Of course, the number of people in the world will probably continue to grow too, so you better keep saving.

itable design, maybe in the future a single person can make a significant difference in helping others.

YEAR	VALUE OF $2000 SAVED ANNUALLY FOR FIRST 10 YEARS	VALUE OF $2000 SAVED ANNUALLY FOR 55 YEARS
10	$35,097	$35,097
20	$109,007	$144,140
30	$338,560	$482,665
40	$1,051,417	$1,534,182
50	$3,265,853	$4,800,036
55	$5,755,550	$8,472,010

CHART 1.1

WHAT IF A PERSON SAVES AND INVESTS $2,000 MORE THAN ONCE?

We looked at a $2,000 one-time savings growing to $1,000,000 in a little less than 55 years. What if you saved $2,000 a year for 10 years? What would it be worth? What if you saved $2,000 per year until you retired, let's say at 55 years of age? Chart 1.1 shows those calculations, again using a 12% annual compound rate of return.

A 15-year-old could be a millionaire at age 55 by saving $2,000 per year for 10 years, 15 years earlier than if he or she saved $2,000 once. Saving $2,000 per year, every year, would allow the 15-year-old to be a millionaire at age 51.

In the first example, our 15-year-old would have accumulated $5,755,550 by age 70; in the second example, $8,472,010. Hopefully these examples have shown you the importance of saving and investing regularly early in life and employing the power of compound interest.

Hard work is a more important indicator of success than talent.

▌▌

Wʜᴀᴛ ɪꜱ Wᴇᴀʟᴛʜʏ?
Hᴏᴡ Mᴜᴄʜ Iꜱ ᴀ Mɪʟʟɪᴏɴ Dᴏʟʟᴀʀꜱ Wᴏʀᴛʜ?

Hᴏᴡ Mᴜᴄʜ Iꜱ Wᴇᴀʟᴛʜʏ?

WILL Rogers once said something to the effect that if you want to be rich, put all your money in stocks. When they go up, sell them; if they don't go up—don't buy them. That is great advice but obviously a little difficult to execute after the fact. Most everyone would like to have a million dollars or feel rich. Let's examine what it actually means to be wealthy.

Normally, being considered a millionaire is a result of having a net worth of more than one million dollars. Net worth is equal to the value of assets (what a person owns) minus the amount of liabilities (what a person owes).

Assets are stocks, bank deposits, bonds, houses, cars, etc. Liabilities, or debts, would be the outstanding balance of any loans for a home, car, or other borrowings including credit cards. Therefore, net worth is just what it implies— the net of a person's worth.

9

As an example, let's say John saved and accumulated $20,000 in his bank account. For simplicity's sake, let's assume that this is all of his assets and that he has no debts (owes no money). John would have $20,000 of assets and zero liabilities and therefore a $20,000 net worth (see Chart 2.1). Now, let's assume John decided to buy a small house costing $50,000. He didn't have $50,000, but he had good credit and enough money to make a required $10,000 down payment on the house (20% of the cost), and his bank loaned him the rest of the purchase price, or $40,000. John now has more assets and also more liabilities, but he still has the same net worth (see Chart 2.1).

JOHN'S FINANCIAL STATEMENT	
Assets	**Amount**
Bank Deposit $20,000	
Total Assets	$20,000
Liabilities	
None	
Total Liabilities	0
Net Worth	$20,000

JOHN'S REVISED FINANCIAL STATEMENT		
Assets		**Amount**
Bank Deposit	$10,000	
House	$50,000	
Total Assets		$60,000
Liabilities		
Bank Loan	($40,000)	
Total Liabilities		($40,000)
Net Worth		$20,000

CHART 2.1

Being a millionaire is not what it used to be, but it is still much more than you might think. According to *Forbes*[4] magazine, you need a net worth of $368,000 to be in the top 10% of all the wealthy people in the United States

---

[4] "The Billionaire Next Door," *Forbes*, October 11, 1999.

today. In addition to net worth, another significant factor in determining the wealth of an individual or family is net income, or how much you earn annually. In most parts of the country, an income of $45,000 or more would put you in the top 50% of all household incomes. This $45,000 is the lower range of what is considered upper middle class for 17 million households, or one-sixth of all the households in the United States. If you had a million dollars in investable assets that could potentially produce $75,000 of annual income, that would put you in the top one-sixth of all households' income without working.

Today, there are five million U.S. households with a million-dollar net worth, which is less than 5% of all households. That number is expected to quadruple in 10 years to 20 million households.

The surprising statistic is not how many families have a million-dollar net worth, but how many have a zero net worth and earn less than $15,000 per year. People with a zero net worth have not followed the plan of this book by saving early in life. The number of families in the latter category is approximately 20 million households, or about 20% of all households.

How much does it take to be rich? According to *Barron's* magazine,[5] being rich requires $2 million today. That $2 million invested conservatively would earn 5% income, which could provide $100,000 of annual income. This is

---

[5] Harold Semetor, "Are You Rich Yet?", *Barron's*, September 20, 1999.

very close to the 95th percentile of all individual taxpayers for the year 1999 based on adjusted gross income. The exact figure is $101,141. The idea is that if you could earn enough income from investments alone to be in the top 5% of all individual taxpayers you would be rich.

According to *Barron's*, you would need $4.55 million of investable assets to be very rich. Conservatively, that amount could produce $227,546 of income, which would place you in the top 1% of all taxpayers.

U.S. FAMILIES 1999 STUDY		
	Net Worth	Income
Top 1%	N/A	$227,000 and above
Top 5%	$1,000,000 and above	$100,000 and above
Top 10%	$368,000 and above	N/A
Top 16%	N/A	$75,000 and above
Top 50%	N/A	$45,000 and above
	N/A	N/A
Bottom 20%	$0 or negative	$15,000 or less

N/A= Not Applicable

CHART 2.2

ATTRIBUTES OF THE TOP 1% OF THE WEALTHY

U.S. Trust, one of the largest banks in the United States, did an eight-year study targeting the top 1% of taxpayers. Seventy-two percent of this group had a net worth of more than $1 million. Approximately 20% had a net worth of more than $5 million. How did they get so rich? They worked hard, stayed married, saved a lot, and invested wisely. Also important to their success was intelligence, good career choices, special skills, and encouragement from their spouses.

Although this book is mainly about saving a lot and investing wisely, I tell students at seminars that there is absolutely no substitute in life for hard work. It is the single most important indicator of success in life, even more important than talent. Not to say that talent isn't important, but given the choice of one or the other, hard work trumps talent. The optimum situation is obviously God-given talent combined with hard work, an unbeatable combination.

The majority of the wealthy in this study said their fortunes came from their own business or professional practices, while another one-third worked for big companies. Less than 10% listed inheritance as the reason for their wealth. On an age basis, 55% were in their 40s and 50s; 19% were in their 30s; the rest were over 60.

When you examine their income, an average of 42% of this money goes to taxes, and the remaining money is used as shown in Chart 2.3.

WEALTHY HOUSEHOLD BUDGET BREAKDOWN	
Housing, Utility, and Maintenance	23%
Food, Clothing	16%
Vacations and Travel	12%
Children's Expenses	8%
Charitable Contributions	8%
Healthcare and Insurance	6%
Savings and Investments	27%

CHART 2.3

Their 27% for savings and investments is about 15 times the national savings rate of 1.8%, which helps explain why they are rich.

Smart investing was also significant. Chart 2.4 shows a breakdown of the portfolio of this very rich group.

Only 43% of their investments are in stocks, which does not seem extremely aggressive. However, it should be noted that at this time in their lives, preserving or maintaining their wealth might be more significant—or at least equally significant—as growing their wealth, especially for the 60 and over group. That helps explain the relatively conservative nature of their investment portfolio.

WEALTHY PORTFOLIO BREAKDOWN	
Domestic Blue Chip Stocks	19%
Domestic Stock Mutual Funds	8%
Domestic Small-Cap Stocks	10%
Money Market Mutual Funds	9%
Cash Equivalents	15%
U.S. Government Securities	6%
International Stocks	6%
Real Estate	11%
Bond Mutual Funds	2%
Municipal Funds	10%
Corporate Bonds	4%

CHART 2.4

WHAT AMOUNT OF DOLLARS WOULD IT TAKE FOR YOU TO FEEL RICH?		
Dollar Amount to Feel Rich	**1984**	**1999**
$100,000	28%	2%
$250,000	11%	4%
$500,000	17%	7%
$1 million	25%	30%
$3 million	7%	28%
$5 million or more	8%	28%

CHART 2.5

WHAT DOES IT TAKE TO FEEL RICH?

Americans with $50,000-plus of household income were asked that question by *Money*[6] magazine. Their answers are expressed in Chart 2.5.

Only 43% thought $1 million was rich in 1999, compared to 81% in 1984. In 1999, more than half thought it required $3–$5 million to feel rich. With modest and regular saving and investing, these amounts or more can be reached.

TOP FINANCIAL CONCERNS

Interestingly enough, the top three financial concerns in the *Money* magazine survey were: 1) having enough for retirement, 2) medical costs, and 3) education costs.

[6] Suzanne Wooley, "Americans and Their Money," *Money*, December 1999.

Finally, in this same survey, Americans thought the best way to get rich was to invest in real estate or start their own business. Investing in stocks placed third in the survey.

What Does Wealth Do for You?

As a banker for over 28 years, I have worked with a number of people who are quite wealthy. It is interesting to note, and I believe studies will back this up, that most of them appear to be regular Joes. In fact, you would have a hard time picking them out in a crowd as being any different from anyone else. Most of them do not flaunt money but rather use it as a tool to enhance their lives. Yes, wealth can allow a person to buy things such as big houses or fancy cars, but for most wealthy people it provides them security and a certain degree of freedom to do what they enjoy in life. Wealth can also provide for really important things like a child's education, or the ability of one's spouse to stay home while the kids are young, or the choice to invest further in their own business or profession, thereby allowing it to grow more rapidly. Although most wealthy people live comfortably in a nice home in a safe area, many do not spend on extremely luxurious items.

I will never forget letting an elderly farmer into our bank after hours one day. He was unshaven, and his overalls were covered from head to toe with dirt and mud. Based on appearance alone, it would have been easy to think this man was a bum looking for a handout. I let him in and he deposited several hundred thousand dollars in our bank. It turned out this man was, in fact, a very successful and hardworking farmer who owned thousands of acres of farmland. As the old saying goes, you cannot always judge a book by its cover.

WHO WANTS TO BE A MILLIONAIRE?

At the seminars I give to students, I usually ask who is going to be a millionaire someday. Normally one-half to two-thirds of the students will raise their hands. Probably one-third still keep their hands up when I ask who will have $10 million, and a significant number still keep their hands up when I ask who will have $100 million. Usually at least one or two in the crowd still keep their hands up when I ask who will be a billionaire. I usually ask if I can give those students my business card because I would like to have just a part of their future deposit business! I consider this to be very positive for our country, because it shows today's youth are generally very optimistic toward the future. Oh, to be young again!

> **STUDY OF TOP 1% OF WEALTHY**
>
> **Why Are They Wealthy?**
>
> Worked hard, stayed married, saved a lot, and invested wisely. Also intelligence, good career choices, special skills, and encouragement from their spouses.

With the strategies described in this book, reaching the millionaire category at some point in the future should be possible for almost anyone. With ongoing significant savings year after year, many of these people can also reach the very wealthy category.

III

FACTORS THAT MAKE COMPOUNDING WORK

WHY I WROTE THIS BOOK

I HAVE been fascinated with compound interest for almost as long as I can remember. Ten or 15 years ago, I began giving talks on the importance of saving and the power of compound interest to elementary school classes through a local "Partners in Education" program. This program encouraged local businesses to visit the classroom. At the time, I used a rather simple one-sheet handout.

A few years ago, I decided to do a type of evaluation of my own life by listing what was important to me, such as my beliefs, values, and ideas and concepts that I was passionate about. Other than rather obvious ones, such as God, family, truthfulness, moral character, and a few others, one of the concepts that was near the top of my list was the power of compound interest and how little it was understood, especially among young people. When I realized how strongly I felt about this, I asked myself what I could do about it. It was then that I decided to use my 28 years in banking and investments, my certified financial planning degree, and my passion and interest in the subject matter to put together a clear and concise why and how-to book. I hope that I have been successful. You can decide for yourself when you finish the book.

As an aside, listing out what is important to you is a worthwhile exercise that can tell you a lot about yourself—and it may inspire you to write a book.

How Does Compound Interest Work?

Albert Einstein, who most all of us would consider to have been reasonably bright, is quoted as describing compound interest as "the greatest mathematical discovery of all time." I've heard others call it the "eighth wonder of the world," and I agree with both. If Albert Einstein and others felt that strongly about this concept, let's take the time to examine the factors that make compounding work: time and return (interest) and their interaction when you let return earn on top of return.

First, let's understand exactly what compound return (interest) is. Compound interest is interest, or return, earned on an investment that is added back into the investment regularly so that each subsequent period you, the investor, earn interest on the original investment plus the interest earned from all previous periods.

It should also be noted that "interest" and "return" can be considered as two different calculations. Normally, interest rate, or interest, is a fixed rate of return earned or paid on a note, debt, bond, or deposit, and it is less risky. As an example, a bank deposit pays a fixed interest rate. The rate of return, on the other hand, might include interest and any price appreciation from the investment. It would probably be assumed to have a higher degree of risk. Stocks may pay a dividend like an Interest rate, except the rate can fluctuate. Usually the dividend increases plus the stock could grow in price, or appreciate, together creating a rate of return. However, for the purposes of describing compound interest in this book, I have considered the terms interest and return to mean the same thing.

In order to explain compound interest, and for simplicity's sake, let's assume you put $100 in a savings account or money market account that pays 5% compounded annual interest.[7] The calculation is shown in Chart 3.1.

COMPOUNDED INTEREST 5%	
$100.00	Original Deposit
.05 x	Times 5% Interest
$ 5.00	= Interest Earned
$100.00	+ Original Deposit
$105.00	= End of Year Balance

CHART 3.1

[7] In late 2002, interest rates were near all-time lows for the last 40 years, so savings accounts and money market accounts were currently paying much less than 5%—mostly between 1% and 2%. Since this is historically very low, it was assumed there will be time in the future when these accounts pay 5% as they have in the past.

At the end of one year, with $5.00 of interest, you now have $105.00. Now, here is how the compounding begins to work. In the second year, you earn 5% on $105.00, not just on the original $100. Therefore, in the second year, the interest earned is $5.25, as calculated and shown in Chart 3.2. In the third year, $5.51 of interest is earned.

5% AFTER 2 AND 3 YEARS			
$105.00	End-of-Year-One Balance	$110.25	End-of-Year-Two Balance
.05	x 5% Interest	.05	x 5% Interest
$5.25	= Interest Earned	$5.51	= Interest Earned
$105.00	+ End-of-Year-One Balance	$110.25	+ End-of-Year-Two Balance
$110.25	= End-of-Year-Two Balance	$115.76	= End-of-Year-Three Balance

CHART 3.2

Each year, interest is earned on the original deposit plus the interest accumulated or compounded. If you did not compound the interest, or earn interest on interest, you could earn only $5 each year forever. That is not compounding. Or if you took the $5 and spent it each year, you would never be able to compound the interest. Therefore, in year 10 or year 50, you would still be earning only $5 each year.

Compounding as we have shown it so far seems to work rather slowly, but let's carry it out a number of years and see what happens (Chart 3.3).

50 YEARS AT 5%	
Year	End-of-Year Balance on $100
1	$105.00
2	$110.25
5	$115.26
4	$121.55
5	$127.62
10	$162.88
15	$207.89
20	$265.32
25	$338.63
30	$432.19
40	$703.99
50	$1,146.74

CHART 3.3

Notice that if you took 5% interest and saved it separately for 15 years without compounding, you would have $100 + [$5 x (15 years) = $75] = $175. By compounding the interest, though, you have $207.89. Given time, compounding can be a very powerful tool. In fact, it is an exponential or geometric function. That means that as you chart time against value, it grows exponentially, as shown in Chart 3.4.

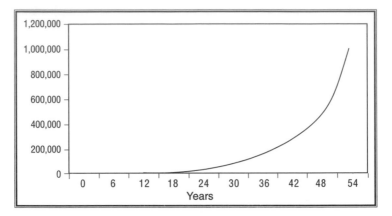

CHART 3.4

50 YEARS AT 10%	
Year	End-of-Year Balance on $100
1	$110.00
2	$121.00
3	$133.10
4	$146.41
5	$161.05
10	$259.37
15	$417.72
20	$672.75
25	$1,033.47
30	$1,744.94
40	$4,525.92
50	$11,739.08

CHART 3.5

Now, let's look at a 10% interest rate, shown in Chart 3.5, on the same $100 investment. (Please realize that a money market account won't pay an interest rate this high.) By year 15, the 10% grows to more than twice what 5% does; at year 30, it grows by approximately four times more; and at 50 years, it is 10 times more.

FREQUENCIES OF COMPOUNDING PERIODS

See how much faster the same $100 grows at 10% instead of 5%? The interest rate or rate of return obviously makes a huge difference.

Although it is a relatively small factor in this concept, interest can be—and is, in many cases—compounded more frequently than yearly. If 5% was compounded semiannually, the calculation works like that shown in Chart 3.6.

$100.00	Original investment
x .05	Annual interest rate
$5.00	Annual interest
Divided by 2	1/2 of year
$2.50	Interest for first 6 months
+ $100.00	Original investment
$102.50	Investment balance plus interest after 6 months
x .05	Annual interest rate
$5.125	Annual interest
Divided by 2	1/2 of year
$2.5625	Second 6-month interest
+ $102.50	6-month investment balance
$105.0625	Balance at year end

CHART 3.6

Compounding the same rate of interest semiannually earns $5.06, six cents more on the $100 than 5% compounded annually. This is called the annual percentage yield or APY. More frequent compounding also increases the APY, as shown in Chart 3.7.

5% COMPOUNDED VARIOUS WAYS	
Rate 5%	APY
Annual Compound	5.00%
Semi-Annual Compound	5.06%
Quarterly	5.09%
Monthly	5.12%
Daily	5.13%

CHART 3.7

The more frequent the compounding, the higher the return. However, as shown in Chart 3.7, the increase in yield is minimal beyond monthly compounding. Using a 5% interest rate and compounding annually calculates to an APY of 5%. Compounding 5% semiannually results in an APY of 5.06%. More frequent compounding continues to increase the APY, but by smaller differences as the frequency increases.

COMPONENTS OF COMPOUND INTEREST: TIME AND RETURN

Now that you understand compound interest, let's look at the two important components of compounding—time and return.

TIME

Given enough time, any amount of money compounded will grow exponentially to infinity. In our 50-year example, 10% compounded $100 to $11,739. In the same 50 years, 5% compounded $100 to only $1,146. The 5% could eventually compound to $11,739, but it would take 97.67 years instead of 50, almost twice as long as it takes 10% to grow to that amount.

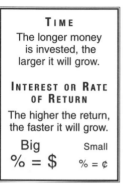

TIME
The longer money
is invested, the
larger it will grow.

INTEREST OR RATE OF RETURN
The higher the return,
the faster it will grow.

Big   Small
% = $ % = ¢

RETURN

The higher the compound return, the more quickly exponential growth occurs. The argument above works in reverse.

Compounding is the concept that combines time and return in a very explosive way, like a spark and dynamite. Without compounding, the graph of the accumulated value

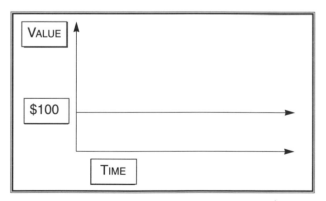

of $100 at 5% or any interest rate would look like the one on the preceding page. Without compounding, the value of your $100 investment would never grow past $100 because each

> **COMPOUNDING**
>
> The process of combining interest with time and allowing interest to grow and accumulate on interest.

year you theoretically spend the $5. Allowing return or interest to accumulate and be paid on interest is a very powerful concept.

REMEMBER THESE TWO FACTORS

The longer the time, the more powerful the effect of compounding. Likewise, the higher the return, the more powerful the effect of compounding.

"The new law of the land is now the Rule of 72!"

IV

THE RULE OF 72

THE MICHAEL JORDAN OF FINANCIAL CONCEPTS

TO make the point of the power of compound interest to students and young adults, many times I start my seminars on this subject by asking students, "Who is the best athlete of all time?" I usually receive many different answers: Tiger Woods, Shaquille O'Neal, Babe Ruth, and many others.

By far the most frequent answer I receive to the question of who is the best athlete of all time is Michael Jordan. This is the answer I'm looking for, because many young adults, like my own kids, idolize Jordan and believe, probably rightly so, that he is the best of all time. I conclude the discussion of the best athlete of all time and bring it back to compound interest by saying, "Compound interest is the Michael Jordan of financial concepts." That opens students' eyes and ears because they realize Jordan is the best of the best and, therefore, so is the power of compound interest.

Sometimes I get some interesting responses to this question. Boys will answer with the young and attractive tennis star Anna Kournikova. I respond that I am asking for "best" not "best-looking." One high school student responded to my question with the name of "Logan Biggerstaff." Since I had never heard of that name, I said, "I'm assuming that is you." He answered with a little grin, "Yeah, that's right," and all his friends laughed. I am anxiously waiting to see if he becomes the best athlete of all time.

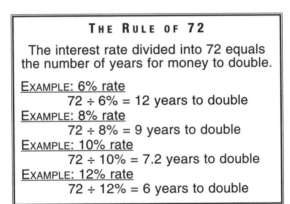

THE RULE OF 72

The interest rate divided into 72 equals the number of years for money to double.

EXAMPLE: 6% rate
$$72 \div 6\% = 12 \text{ years to double}$$
EXAMPLE: 8% rate
$$72 \div 8\% = 9 \text{ years to double}$$
EXAMPLE: 10% rate
$$72 \div 10\% = 7.2 \text{ years to double}$$
EXAMPLE: 12% rate
$$72 \div 12\% = 6 \text{ years to double}$$

HOW QUICKLY CAN MONEY DOUBLE IN VALUE?

To see how compound interest works, you don't have to have a sophisticated financial calculator or a dozen pencils and a ream of paper to do the calculations. All you really need is to understand The Rule of 72.

The Rule of 72 is a financial rule that everyone should learn because it is a quick and easy way to estimate how quickly an investment can double given a particular interest rate. Anyone can figure how fast money can grow and compound without having to use a financial calculator. This rule is important because it allows a person to understand the interaction between time, interest, and compounding of interest—and how they work together to make money grow.

The Rule of 72 is as follows: The interest rate or return divided into 72 equals approximately the number of years it takes money to double. Alternately, the number of years divided into 72 equals approximately the interest rate required for money to double in that number of years.

Let's look at some examples. For simplicity, we'll use numbers that divide into 72 evenly. With a 6% interest rate, it would take 12 years for money to double (72 ÷ 6% = 12 years). Likewise, if you want to know the interest rate required for money to double in 12 years, divide 12 into 72 to get 6% (72 ÷ 12 years = 6%).

Notice that if you use a 12% annual compounded rate instead of 6%, it takes six years for the money to double rather than 12 (72 ÷ 12% = 6 years). A 12% annual compounded return can double an investment in six years; whereas at a 6% annual compound rate, it takes 12 years. So if you invest $2,000 at 6%, it would take 12 years to grow to $4,000. If, however, you are able to invest it at 12% annually, it will take only 6 years to grow to $4,000.

When the power of time is added into this equation, the concept becomes extremely interesting and important. If

6% Vs. 12%			
COMPOUNDING AT 6% NUMBER OF YEARS	VALUE OF $2,000	COMPOUNDING AT 12% NUMBER OF YEARS	VALUE OF $2,000
0	$2,000	0	$2,000
12	$4,000	6	$4,000
24	$8,000	12	$8,000
36	$16,000	18	$16,000
48	$32,000	24	$32,000
60	$64,000	30	$64,000
72	$128,000	36	$128,000
84	$256,000	42	$256,000
96	$512,000	48	$512,000
108	$1,024,000	54	$1,024,000
		60	$2,054,000
		66	$4,108,000
		72	$8,216,000
		78	$16,434,000
		84	$32,868,000
		90	$65,736,000
		96	$131,472,000
		102	$262,944,000
		108	$525,888,000

CHART 4.1

a 12% compounded annual interest rate can double to $2,000 in six years, it can do the same in another six years and so on indefinitely. Therefore, if $2,000 grows to $4,000 in six years, then it grows not another $2,000 in six years, but from $4,000 to $8,000. Remember, you are doubling an already doubled figure. See Chart 4.1.[8]

---

[8] This chart does not reduce the compounded amount by potential income taxes.

You can see in this chart that at 6%, $2,000 would grow to only $64,000 in 60 years. At 6%, it would actually take 108 years, using The Rule of 72, to exceed $1,000,000. Obviously, no one has 108 years to invest, which shows why the interest rate is important along with time. At 12%, using The Rule of 72, $2,000 can double to $1,024,000 in 54 years—half the time of 6%. Many adults don't have 54 years for that to happen, but a 15-year-old certainly does, as does a 20-year-old. A 15-year-old who saves $2,000 can invest it at 12% compounded annually and expect more than one million dollars by age 69.

To look at the bigger picture, in the same time it takes $2,000 at 6% to double repeatedly to more than one million dollars, that same $2,000 at 12% is worth approximately $525,888,000. That is the power of compounding.

As discussed in the previous chapter, the three secrets here are 1) Give time a chance to work. Every few years can double money one more time. That is why it is so important to save early in life. 2) Higher rates of return make a huge difference. Twice the rate means half the time for money to double. 3) Interest or return must be left in the pot to be allowed to earn interest on interest.

Understanding the significance of The Rule of 72 along with the long-term results from its use is an eye-opening experience.

"Son, I've decided to make you a millionaire with this small amount to start, all you have to do is leave it alone and let it grow."

V

THE INVESTMENT
OF CHOICE

LONG-TERM PERFORMANCE OF VARIOUS INVESTMENTS

THERE are two parts to becoming a millionaire. The first part is saving early in life to use time to your advantage. The second part is making a wise investment that safely maximizes your return over long periods of time.

Chart 5.1, from Ibbotson and Associates, shows the growth of $100 for various investment classes from 1926 to the end of 2001.

During that time, $100 invested in treasury bills or cash equivalents would have grown to $1,720 for a 3.8% average annual return. This was slightly better than inflation, which compounded $100 at 3.1% to $987. A hundred dollars invested in long-term bonds grew at a 5.6% rate to $5,066. Stocks, as measured by large and small stock, grew at 12.8% and 17.4% annually on average.[9] Large capitalization

---

[9] This is an average return. The compound return or geometric return is more accurate for our purposes of compounding. The geometric return for large stocks is 10.7%. The geometric return for small stocks is 12.5%.

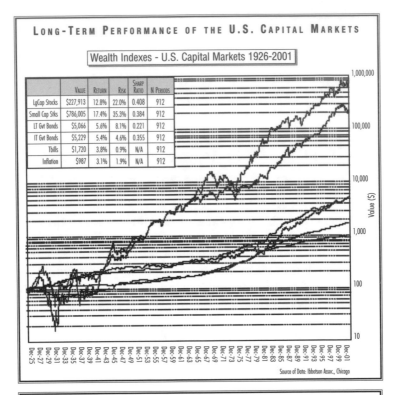

LONG-TERM PERFORMANCE OF THE U.S. CAPITAL MARKETS

Wealth Indexes - U.S. Capital Markets 1926-2001

	VALUE	RETURN	RISK	SHARP RATIO	N PERIODS
LgCap Stocks	$227,913	12.8%	22.0%	0.408	912
Small Cap Stks	$786,005	17.4%	35.3%	0.384	912
LT Gvt Bonds	$5,066	5.6%	8.1%	0.221	912
IT Gvt Bonds	$5,229	5.4%	4.6%	0.355	912
Tbills	$1,720	3.8%	0.9%	N/A	912
Inflation	$987	3.1%	1.9%	N/A	912

Source of Data: Ibbotson Assoc., Chicago

CHART 5.1 INFORMATION

This chart shows the growth of a $100 investment since January 1926 in each of the different domestic asset classes. The chart shows the power of compound growth over very long time frames. The chart also shows that over longer time frames, higher risk assets such as equities have historically been rewarded with substantially higher growth.

stocks are stocks with a current market capitalization of $10 billion or more. Market capitalization is defined as the number of shares of stock outstanding (owned by share-

holders) times the price per share of the stock. It is a
measure of how investors value the entire company or what
the market would pay to own the entire company. As an
example, a company with one billion
shares outstanding and a price per
share of $30 would have a market
capitalization of $30 billion. It would,
therefore, be a large capitalization
stock because its capitalization is
over $10 billion.

> 12% is the approximate
> compounded return
> of stocks over the
> last 75 years.

A hundred dollars invested in large capitalization stocks in
1926 grew to $227,913 by 2001, and $100 invested in
small capitalization stocks grew to a whopping $786,005.
Imagine having $100 invested in small capitalization
stocks in 1926. It would be worth $786,005. A mere $1,000
would be worth almost $8 million.

RETURN VS. RISK

It should be noted that stocks outperformed inflation, on
average, by more than 10% every year. You can see this
on Chart 5.1. Chart 5.2 shows the relationship between
risk and reward. Returns for various types of investments
are indicated on the vertical axis of the chart. Risk is
measured using standard deviation, a measure of volatility
(i.e., up and down price movement). Volatility, or risk of price
movement, is measured on the horizontal axis, with higher
volatility the further you go to the right of the chart. The chart
shows that small stocks had the highest average return with
an average yearly return of 17.4% and are, therefore, highest

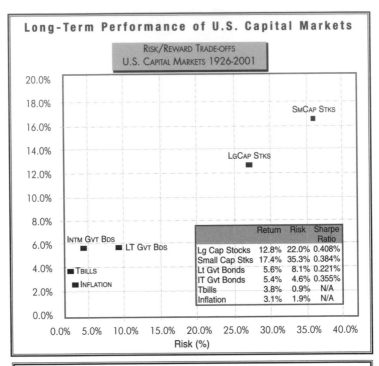

Long-Term Performance of U.S. Capital Markets

RISK/REWARD TRADE-OFFS
U.S. CAPITAL MARKETS 1926-2001

	Return	Risk	Sharpe Ratio
Lg Cap Stocks	12.8%	22.0%	0.408%
Small Cap Stks	17.4%	35.3%	0.384%
Lt Gvt Bonds	5.6%	8.1%	0.221%
IT Gvt Bonds	5.4%	4.6%	0.355%
Tbills	3.8%	0.9%	N/A
Inflation	3.1%	1.9%	N/A

Risk (%)

CHART 5.2

Investment theory and historical capital market return data suggest that, over long periods of time, there is a relationship between the level of risk assumed and the level of return that can be expected in an investment program. In general, higher risk (i.e., volatility of return) is associated with higher return. This chart shows the historical average return and risk for stocks and bonds since 1926. (The year 1926 is the inception date for the domestic stock and bond market indexes.)

Source of Data: Ibbotson Assoc. Chicago

on the chart. Small stocks also had the most volatility with a standard deviation of 35.3% and are, therefore, farthest to the right. Typically, more risk means more return.

With the first bear market in the United States since 1987 beginning in 2000, simultaneously with the first recession in a number of years in 2001, many people were scared of investing in the market at year-end 2001 because they were worried the market would go down further. I believe

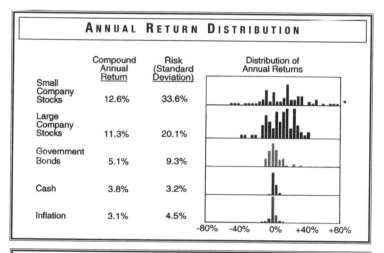

that market corrections provide a real opportunity for a long-term investor.

To understand why, take a look at Chart 5.3. This chart shows the distribution of annual returns over the last 73-year period ending in 1999. If you look at small stocks, their annual returns have ranged from down 60% to over 100%. Most people would not want to be down 60% in a year. Investing following a significant downturn actually makes sense because, given time, the market will have to bounce back further to reach its

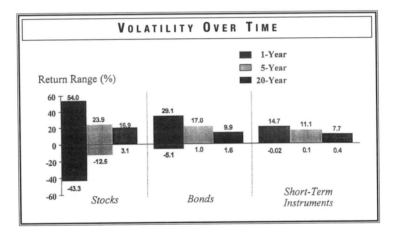

VOLATILITY OVER TIME

Return Range (%)

■ 1-Year
▨ 5-Year
■ 20-Year

Stocks: 54.0, 23.9, 16.9, 3.1, -12.5, -43.3
Bonds: 29.1, 17.0, 9.9, 1.0, 1.6, -5.1
Short-Term Instruments: 14.7, 11.1, 7.7, -0.02, 0.1, 0.4

CHART 5.4
Source: *Stocks, Bonds, Bills and Inflation 1996 Yearbook.* [SBBI] Ibbotson Associates, Chicago (annually updates work by Roger G. Ibbotson and Rex A. Sinquefield). Used with permission. All rights reserved. This chart is a graphic representation of the historical annual, rolling 5-year-period, and rolling 20-year-period returns for the S&P 500, intermediate-term government bonds, and U.S. Treasury bills for the period 1926-1995. This is not intended to imply the past or future performance of any investment.

historic average. Unfortunately, it is nearly impossible to know when the market has reached its low. But if you have time on your side, you can minimize the potential for loss.

RISK DECREASES WITH TIME

Chart 5.4 shows how volatility diminishes over time. From 1926 to 1995, stocks (big and small combined) were down as much as 43% in one year. But in any five-year period the maximum decrease was 12.5%; and in any 20-year period, the minimum return was 3.1% annually. The ability to wait through ups and downs in the market allows you to end up ahead; and over time, you should reach the historic norm.

The important thing to remember is that volatility (risk) is minimized the longer you can wait. If you invest $1.00 today and it goes down to $.50 tomorrow and up to $2.00 in two days, you haven't lost $.50 unless you had to sell the second day. If you wait until the third day, you have a sizeable profit.

INVESTING REGULARLY (DOLLAR AVERAGING) LOWERS RISK

Studies have shown that a downturn in the market can actually help you in the long-term if you are investing periodically (called dollar averaging). If the market goes down, you will be able to buy more shares at that time for every dollar spent.

Let's look at the price of an imaginary company we will call ABC Company over a 6-year period as listed on the next page.

ABC COMPANY	
YEAR	PRICE
1	$10
2	$ 5
3	$10
4	$30
5	$15
6	$20

If you bought the stock in year one at $10 and held it to year six, you doubled your money to $20 and, therefore, earned a 12% compounded return (The Rule of 72). If you happened to buy at the low in year two at $5 per share, you did great and were lucky, as your stock grew from $5 to $20 in five years. If, however, you bought in year four at $30 and held to year six at $20, you have lost 50% of your investment and were unlucky.

However, if we assume you invested $60 per year every year, here is what would happen:

YEAR	PRICE	NUMBER OF SHARES PURCHASED	TOTAL DOLLARS INVESTED
1	$10	6	$ 60
2	$ 5	12	$ 60
3	$10	6	$ 60
4	$30	2	$ 60
5	$15	4	$ 60
6	$20	3	$ 60
Total		33	$ 360

CHART 5.5

The average price during that six-year period is 10+5+15+30+15+20 = 90 ÷ 6 = $15 per share. However, if you bought every year, your average price was $10.90 per share ($360 invested at $60 per year ÷ 33 shares purchased), which is much lower than the overall average price. The reason your average purchase price ($10.90) is significantly lower than the average price ($15) is because you have invested the same dollar amount each year, which allowed you to purchase more shares when the price was low. Although dollar averaging does not ensure that you will buy only at the lowest price, it does ensure that you will not buy only at the highest price. More important, your average purchase price will be lower than the average price. Therefore, this is considered an advantageous way to invest for long-term investors. We will cover more on dollar averaging later as it relates to the discipline of saving and investing regularly.

> The S&P 500® (a registered trademark of Standard & Poor's) is an unmanaged index of common stock prices. Data is historical, and yield, share price, and return will vary. You may have a gain or loss when you sell your shares. Past performance is no guarantee of future results. An investor cannot invest directly in the index.

The best strategy is to be fully invested in stocks and periodically purchase more.

MARKET TIMING, OR INVESTING AT THE LOW, IS HIGHLY UNLIKELY

When the market has had an extended up period, many times people say, "If the market is too high, maybe I should wait until it drops and invest then." That is a good thought, but in practice it does not work well. Chart 5.6 shows the annual return in the market over a 10-year period from 1986 to 1995. Being fully invested for all 2,526 trading days produces a 14.8% annual return. At the other extreme—being out of the market for the 40 best days in that period—the return lowered to 2.5% annually.

Market Timing Minus Best Days

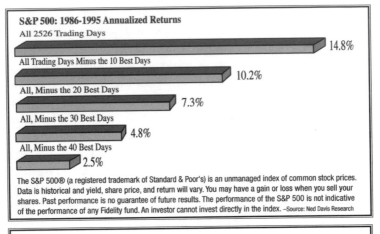

S&P 500: 1986-1995 Annualized Returns

All 2526 Trading Days — 14.8%

All Trading Days Minus the 10 Best Days — 10.2%

All, Minus the 20 Best Days — 7.3%

All, Minus the 30 Best Days — 4.8%

All, Minus the 40 Best Days — 2.5%

The S&P 500® (a registered trademark of Standard & Poor's) is an unmanaged index of common stock prices. Data is historical and yield, share price, and return will vary. You may have a gain or loss when you sell your shares. Past performance is no guarantee of future results. The performance of the S&P 500 is not indicative of the performance of any Fidelity fund. An investor cannot invest directly in the index. –Source: Ned Davis Research

CHART 5.6

If you think the market is about to tank, it's always tempting to pull your money out and wait on the sidelines until you feel stocks have bottomed out. But consider the accompanying chart. If you had stayed fully invested in stocks (as measured by the S&P 500) from January 1, 1986, to December 31, 1995—including the dark days of 1987—you would have earned annual returns of 14.8%. If you had tried to time the ups and downs of the market, you would have risked missing out on days that registered some of the biggest gains. And the more good days you missed, the lower your portfolio's returns.

Chart 5.7 shows the historical performance from 1926 to 1999 if you were able to miss the worst one month and if you were able to miss the worst 12 months.

Worst Months

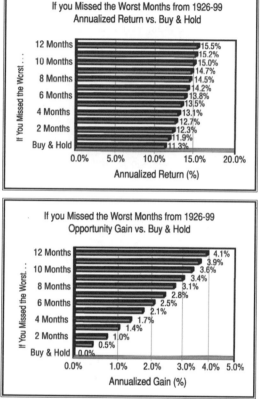

CHART 5.7

The annual return increases four-tenths of 1% if you had missed the worst month and 4.2% if you had missed the worst 12 months in that 62-year period. Everyone would like to miss the worst periods, but the problem with timing is that no one

CHART 5.7

The previous chart shows the worst-case result from a market timing perspective—results from perfectly bad timing. These results show an equally extreme case—results if you switched from the S&P 500 to T-bills and happened to miss the worst months during the period 1926-99. This is perfectly good market timing. An investor who remained invested throughout the period (888 months) would have earned an annualized return of 11.3%.

If the investor happened to miss the worst month out of this period, the annualized return would have been increased to 11.9% (or an annualized opportunity gain of +0.6%). Missing progressively more of the worst performing months has progressively better results on the realized annual return.

One further observation from these charts is the asymmetry of the results. Note that missing the 12 worst months had a bigger annualized opportunity gain of +4.1% while missing the 12 best months would have led to an annualized opportunity loss of -3.4%.

knows for sure when the market will go up or down. You can miss the boat while waiting on the shore for a correction that may never come. Over time, this dollar-averaging technique will ensure that you have not invested everything at the high point or peak. However, if your plan is to invest just once do it now and give time a chance to work in your favor.

WHAT IF THE MARKET GOES DOWN?

In a study of bear markets since 1970, defined as markets where stocks dropped 10% or more in value from their high or peak value to their low or trough value, the worst of these was from December 1972 to September 1974 in which the S&P 500 dropped 42.6%. The longest time it took to recover all the loss from each bear market was 21 months from the 1973-1974 period. In other words, since 1970, if you invested in the overall stock market at the very worst time possible, it took only 21 months to recover all you had lost. From March of 2000 to July 2002 the S&P dropped 48.7%. At the time of this publication, it was unclear how long it would take to recover this loss, but history has shown that the market can recover past losses very quickly. Therefore investing near a market low is advisable for the long run.

WHAT ARE THE LONG-TERM EXPECTATIONS FOR THE MARKET?

The bear market beginning in March of 2000 dampened investor confidence in stocks and at midyear 2002, stocks were still not cheap based on historic norms. However many experts predict the market will go significantly higher. Wharton College professor Jeremy Siegel in his book, *Stocks for the Long Run*, expects stocks to provide an inflation-adjusted average return of between 5% and 8%. In his book, he tracks stock performance back to 1802. He found that for any significant holding period, especially 10 years or more, stocks significantly outperformed bonds and inflation. See Chart 5.8.

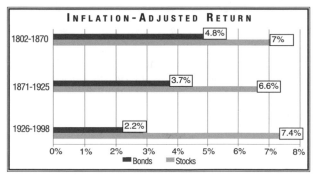

CHART 5.8

49

Harry Dent, author of a business best seller, *The Roaring 2000s*, and its sequel, *The Roaring 2000s Investor*, predicts the market will rise for another decade. Dent's theory for stock market growth is based on demographic trends. He has shown that the Dow seems to move in step with the 46½-year-olds in the United States. See Chart 5.9.

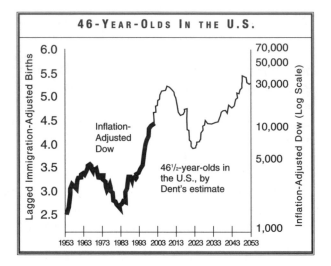

CHART 5.9

Dent developed his spending wave model in 1993 and uses it to predict the Dow at 41,000 by 2008. His logic is that people in that age group tend to be at the peak of their lifetime spending and, therefore, help create demand and increasing economic growth, pushing the market up. Dent believes the market will fall after 2008 when the number of 46½-year-olds begins to decline.

Journalist Jones Glassman and former Federal Reserve economist Kevin Hassett predict Dow 36,000 in a book with the same name, which is a huge advance from current values. Many experts believe the S&P 500 is expensive based on its 2001 near year-end, 23-time price-to-earnings ratio compared to its historic average of 14. This means the market is more expensive relative to its earnings than it has been on average.[10] Glassman and Hassett believe stocks may be worth 100 times price-to-earnings ratio. Their theory is that once investors understand that stocks are safer than bonds for larger holding periods—as the historical data suggests—the equity premium for risk will vanish and stocks will rise dramatically.

A more conservative view for stock returns for the future comes from Roger Ibbotson of Ibbotson and Associates in the April 2002 issue of *The Journal of Financial Planning*. Ibbotson and Associates is the firm that is considered the expert in calculating financial returns. Mr. Ibbotson discussed large stock returns only, which have compounded at 10.7% over the last 75 years ending in 2001. Small stock returns, as you might remember, have compounded at 12.5%. Ibbotson said 4.9% of the historic return came from annual earnings growth, 4.3% came from historic

---

[10] The price-to-earnings ratio, or P/E, is a ratio that relates the price of a stock or index to its earnings. If ABC Company's stock earned $1.00 per share and its price was $10 per share, the price-to-earnings ratio could be 10 ($10 price divided by $1.00 earnings). A $20 price with the same earnings would be a 20 price-to-earnings ratio ($20 price divided by $1.00 earnings). A lower rate is generally considered a better value or a better buy. Remember, though, that the price doesn't have to come down for the ratio to improve. If earnings increase, the ratio becomes lower also. If ABC Company's stock sells at $20 with $1.00 earnings for a 20 P/E ratio and its earnings grow to $2, its P/E ratio drops to 10 ($20 price divided by $2 earnings).

dividends, and approximately 1.25% came from price earning multiple expansion (prices moved slightly higher relative to their earnings). Going forward, Mr. Ibbotson does not see additional multiple expansion and, therefore, predicts a 9.5% compounded return for large stocks, a 4% risk premium to an expected 5.4% treasury bond yield, an investment which is considered to have little or no risk. Although he doesn't mention small stock, it is assumed that they would carry a nearly 2% higher return than large stocks, as they have historically. This would mean small stocks would earn approximately 11.5% compounded, a 6% premium over low-risk treasury bond yields.

WHY OTHER INVESTMENTS ARE NOT AS GOOD AS STOCKS

What about other investments like commodities, real estate, timber, gold, collectibles, etc.? Historically, none of the above has performed as well as stocks. Additionally, stocks have a high degree of liquidity, which means you can buy in and sell out quickly at little cost or markup. Many large stocks trade at a cost of a few pennies per share depending on the size of the trade. Compare that to collectibles that may have a 100% markup between dealer cost and retail. Additionally, many collectible markets are not readily accessible, and you may have no way to guarantee fair prices. But publicly traded stocks can be sold at any time and have a readily ascertainable price via market quotes many times a day.

STOCKS ARE AN INVESTMENT IN AMERICA'S FUTURE

The most important part of stocks is that the owner of U.S. stock is making a long-term investment in the continued growth of our economy and our capitalistic society. Money naturally flows where it can be used most profitably for the highest return. The U.S. stock market is a long-term proxy for free enterprise, American ingenuity, and know-how. Historically, over the long-term, stocks have been the most profitable investment choice available. Stocks have risk (volatility), but that is greatly reduced if you invest regularly and for long periods of time. There is every reason to believe the long-term future of the American economy, and therefore the performance of the stock market, will be just as good in the future as it has been in the past.

MY OWN EXPERIENCE WITH STOCKS

I started to work in a bank as a trainee in 1974, right out of college at the age of 22. The then chairman of the board, Edgerton Welch, and his son, Bill Welch, the president of the bank, took me under their wings with advice and guidance. As I began my career with the bank, one of the tasks I was assigned was learning and assisting in managing our trust department's own stock funds. Our chairman, who was Mr. Welch to me, had me read the *Value Line Investment Service*, which does an excellent job providing information about stocks.

After a few months of work, I invested $500 of my savings in one of our stock funds in December of that year, and then I added to it regularly as much as I could afford to save. As a training exercise, our chairman sometimes had me figure the daily value of the fund with a pencil, pad, and a calculator. It was especially fun to do this when the market was up and not as much fun when the market was down.

The end of 1974 turned out to be an excellent time to start investing in the market because it was the end of a two-year downturn (bear) market and the start of a very strong upward (bull) market. Incidentally, our managed funds did extremely well in the late '70s, so well that *Forbes* and *Business Week* magazines wrote feature articles about our funds, our investment team (myself included), and our then chairman of the board.

GETTING MY KIDS INTERESTED

About eight years ago, to get my own kids interested in stocks, I put money into an account for them and let them help choose a stock to buy. A stock fund is better than an individual stock, but I wanted to let them use part of the money I deposited for them to develop an interest in the stock market. At the time I did this, my older son, Jared, was about 14; Aaron, my middle child, was 11; and my daughter, Kaylee, was about six. I discussed with them a list of companies that sold or made products or services they knew, used, and liked. Jared chose Nike, Aaron chose Pepsi, and Kaylee chose Mattel—she really liked Barbies. Each year I would show them the annual reports, and I think it helped teach them about stocks. All of these stocks have done reasonably well over the past several years. More recently, the boys talked me into buying them a few shares of WWF Wrestling, which has not done as well yet, but that may be a good learning experience, too.

VI

THE EFFECT OF TAXES AND HOW TO MINIMIZE THEIR EFFECT

TAXES CAN GREATLY REDUCE ACCUMULATION

THE late George Harrison of the Beatles wrote the Beatles song *Taxman*, which has lyrics that say, "If you drive a car, I'll tax the street, if you take a walk, I'll tax your feet." During the peak of the Beatles' popularity in the 1960s, the top tax bracket in Great Britain was approximately 90%. In other words, once they reached a certain income level, they got to keep only 10 cents of every dollar earned! No wonder they were sensitive to taxes!

The tax brackets in the United States are not nearly that high, but are still sizeable. There are federal income taxes, state income taxes, and payroll taxes (Social Security and Medicare) all paid on income, sales tax paid on purchases, property tax paid on real estate and personal property (vehicles), estate and gift taxes paid when money is transferred by gift or death, and more.

Taxes on income can make a huge difference in how much money can accumulate through compounding. Income taxes reduce the amount of money that can be saved and compounded in two ways.

First, taxes are paid when income is earned. For example, Wesley and his wife have both taught school for 10 years and both earn $35,000 for a total of $70,000. They have four children, two of which are in college, and for that and other reasons they can't seem to save any money, even though they have good income. Wesley and his wife know this is a problem.

They decide Wesley will work for the city, managing the city pool in the summer, so that they can begin saving money. He expects to earn $2,000 and save and invest all of his earnings. At Wesley and his wife's income level, we are going to assume that they pay federal and state income taxes at a 32% combined rate.[11] This means when he earns $2,000 he has to pay $640 in income taxes, which means he really has only $1,360 to invest instead of the entire $2,000. For simplicity's sake I am ignoring Social Security and Medicare tax.

The second way income tax reduces accumulation is because a fund's earnings may be taxed as income. Wesley invests the $1,360 into a fully taxable stock fund

---

[11] Combined rate is figured at a federal tax rate of 27% for taxable income for 2002 from $46,700 to $112,850 for married taxpayers filing jointly and an assumed 6% state tax rate. (State taxes vary from state to state.) Also, I have assumed each tax is deductible against the other which lowers the overall tax rate slightly.

that has earned 12% per year on a historical basis. Fully taxable means that this account's earnings will be taxed as earnings are produced. This stock fund buys and sells stock frequently and creates regular annual income and taxes for the owners of the fund, like Wesley. Therefore, let's assume Wesley earns 12% on his investment each year. He will have to pay 32% of that 12% earnings in taxes. Effectively, after taxes, he will earn only 8.16% (12% minus 32% of 12%, or 3.84%).

Taxes when income is earned and taxes on investment earnings together greatly reduce the potential for Wesley's invested money to compound. Let's look at this in Chart 6.1. In the first column, I have used The Rule of 72 to show how money grows to over $1,000,000 in 54 years. In the second column, I have shown what Wesley's investment

YEAR	$2,000 INVESTED 12% GROWTH	$1,360 INVESTED 8.16% RETURN
	(THE RULE OF 72)	
6	$4,000	$2,177
12	$8,000	$3,486
18	$16,000	$5,581
24	$32,000	$8,935
30	$64,000	$14,306
36	$128,000	$22,905
42	$256,000	$36,672
48	$512,000	$58,713
54	$1,024,000	$94,002

CHART 6.1

will be after he pays taxes on his wages and after he pays taxes on his investment earnings. Remember, since Wesley paid $640 in taxes, he has only $1,360 left to invest, not $2,000. Each year when he earns 12%, he must pay 3.84% of his earnings in taxes, leaving him a real return of only 8.16%. Notice what a difference that makes over time in accumulated earnings.

In the same time frame of 54 years, Wesley's money, after paying taxes on his wages and then on his investment earnings annually, grew to only $94,000, less than one-tenth as much as in Column 1—$2,000 growing at 12%! But don't lose hope and stop reading. We have solutions to this dilemma.

WAYS TO REDUCE AND DEFER TAXES: IRAS

Retirement account contributions like the traditional Individual Retirement Account (IRA) are tax deductible[12] from earnings. That means Wesley would not have had to pay taxes on the $2,000 he earned if he invested it into an IRA. Therefore, he could invest all $2,000.

Additionally, if within the structure of an IRA Wesley invested into the same stock fund growing at 12%, his account would be allowed to grow at 12% without any taxes being paid while the money is in the account. Instead, taxes are paid when the money is withdrawn from the IRA. There will be more details about this in a later chapter.

---

[12] Traditional IRAs have income limitations for tax deductions if a person is already participating in a qualified plan such as a profit sharing or pension plan.

Money invested into a relatively new type of retirement account, the Roth IRA, grows tax free even at withdrawal, which is better than the traditional IRA in Wesley's case, preserving his investment return even when he withdraws the funds at retirement. However, unlike the traditional IRA, there is no deduction from wages or earnings when the money is invested into the Roth IRA, so in Wesley's case he would have only the $1,360 to invest rather than the $2,000. The Roth IRA will also be discussed in a lot more detail in a later chapter. Just remember for now that there are ways to invest and minimize taxes and make that $2,000 grow to $1,000,000.

OTHER WAYS TO REDUCE OR DEFER TAXES

Most traditional company retirement accounts, like profit-sharing, pension, and 401(k) plans to name only a few, are tax deductible and have deferred taxes. Additionally, annuities and life insurance also defer taxes, although without a tax deduction for contributions. Further, life insurance is tax-free at death. Investments such as municipal bonds earn interest free of federal tax, and if they are issued in the owner's state of residence, they are also free of state income tax.

Education IRAs and 529 Plans also allow invested money to grow tax free if withdrawn for educational purposes. This will also be discussed in some detail in a later chapter.

Assets with gains (a stock bought at $1,000 and sold at $1,500 would have a gain of $500) that are held for over a year before they are sold are taxed at a lower tax rate, the capital gains rate, rather than the regular income tax rate. For the year 2002, the highest federal capital gains tax rate is 20%, whereas the highest federal income tax rate is 38.6%. For lower bracket taxpayers and for appreciated assets sold after five years, the capital gains tax rate can be as low as 8%. Therefore, holding an appreciated asset rather than selling, thereby deferring tax and allowing growth to compound can also defer gains and tax.

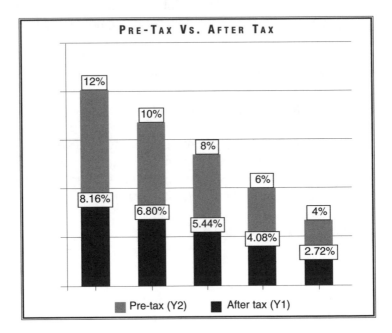

CHART 6.2

CHART 6.2 shows the effective after tax rate returns for various taxable rates of return using a 32% tax bracket as an example. The chart shows that without tax shelters, taxes on investment earnings greatly reduce the actual return you will receive lowering your ability to accumulate wealth substantially.

TAXES LOWER THE COMPOUNDING EFFECT OF MONEY

- Taxes are paid when money is earned.
- Taxes are paid on interest earned on money that is saved or invested.
- Taxes are paid when money is given away (through gift or estate taxes).

A FEW COMMON WAYS TO AVOID OR DEFER TAXES

TRADITIONAL IRA

- No tax when earned (deductible from taxable income)
- Interest is tax-deferred (taxable when the money is taken out)

ROTH IRA

- No deduction from taxable earnings (you are taxed on your salary, wages, or earned income)
- Grows tax-free (even at withdrawal)

All of these are ways to minimize taxes, thereby allowing your money to grow and compound faster. One final comment regarding minimization of taxes is that I am talking legal and legitimate ways to reduce the effect taxes have on accumulation of wealth as opposed to avoidance of taxes by illegal or illegitimate means.

In my banking career, I have had situations where people apply for loans, and their income information from their tax return or financial statement does not support the ability to repay the requested loan. When the applicant is made aware of this, on too many occasions I have heard the answer or the implication of, "I don't report all of my income, if you know what I mean," or "A lot of my business is in cash, so my sales and profits are really higher than they show." In my way of thinking, this is wrong. We have an obligation as citizens to pay what society as a whole has determined is our share to run the country and maintain our freedom and way of life. We do not have to like it, and we can try to change it through representative government, but if it is the law, we owe it and should pay it.

From a lender's standpoint, I have also wanted to chuckle at what these people who do not pay all the taxes they legally owe are saying. In effect, they are telling me, "I am lying to the government and won't pay them what I owe, but I'll tell you the truth and pay you what I owe." Needless to say, that doesn't play well with me or most other bankers.

VII

SAFETY, DIVERSIFICATION

SAFETY IN NUMBERS

THE safest way to invest in the stock market is to buy a well-diversified fund in which you have spread your risk among many different companies. Diversified means you own many different stocks in many different industries or types of business. This is particularly important when you invest for the long-term. The other extreme to owning a well-diversified fund or portfolio is owning stock in only one company. Although owning stock in only one company gives you the opportunity to do better than the market if you are lucky, it also gives you the opportunity to fail miserably if you are unlucky.

The risk associated with an individual stock failing is called unsystematic risk. In other words, an individual stock can move much differently than the overall market. Some studies show that owning as few as eight different stocks takes out most of the unsystematic risk. If you owned Enron stock and it went from $90 per share to zero in 2002, you know what unsystematic risk is. Some recent studies, and most experts and fund managers, suggest owning 50 or more different stocks, and most own several hundred.

For the strategy described in this book to work, it is not necessary to outperform the overall stock market; however, it is necessary not to significantly underperform the overall stock market. Therefore, owning a well-diversified portfolio is extremely important.

OWNING DIFFERENT STYLES OF STOCK INVESTMENTS LOWERS RISK

A study performed by Brinson, Hood, and Bechower in 1986 (and subsequently updated in the '90s) of the returns achieved by pension funds found that asset allocation explained 93.6% of the variance of the portfolio returns, while individual security selection explained only 4.2%. Asset allocation is a way to minimize volatility by owning several different asset groups or types of investments (stocks, bonds, real estate, cash, foreign investments and, in some cases, commodities). Asset allocation lowers volatility over the long-term as compared to an all-stock return, but it would also lower total return. The point here is that individual stock selection is not nearly so important as just owning a diversified stock portfolio.

Some styles of stocks perform better at times than other styles of stocks. One style of stocks known as growth stocks (stocks with rapid growth characteristics but relatively high prices) sometimes outperform another style of stocks known as value stocks (stocks with a low price relative to their earnings, dividends, sales, asset values, etc.). At other times, value stocks outperform growth stocks. See Chart 7.1. When the shaded area is above the middle line, growth has outperformed value. When the shaded area is below, value has outperformed growth.

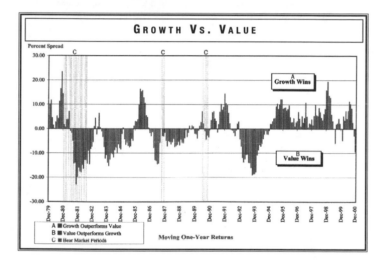

CHART 7.1

Big capitalization stocks sometimes outperform small capitalization; and at other times, small capitalization stocks outperform big capitalization. See Chart 7.2. When the shaded area is above the middle line, large stocks outperformed small stocks, and when it is below, small stocks outperformed large stocks.

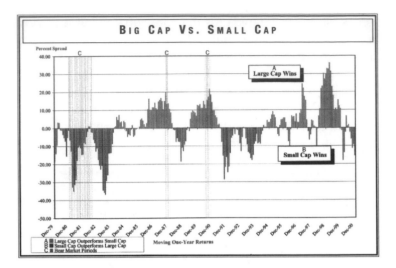

CHART 7.2

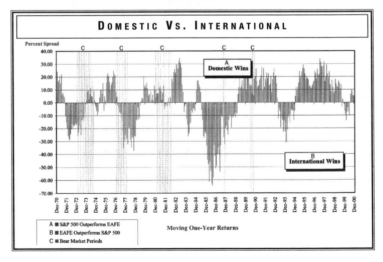

CHART 7.3

Finally, international stocks sometimes outperform domestic company stocks and vice versa. See Chart 7.3.

The long-term return of all of these categories or styles of stocks is similar. But owning all the styles together tends to minimize the volatility, or lower the risk. As an example, assume two asset styles (this same example could be used for certain asset types as well as stock styles); let's call them Type A and Type B, performed over time like the charts below. Both grow to the same ending return, but will get there by different paths. Some investment styles do better in different circumstances, low or high inflation, low or high interest rates, or even booming economies versus economic slowdown.

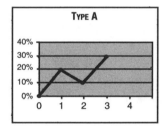
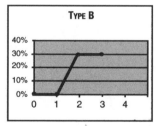

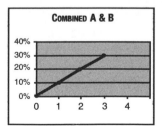

CHART 7.4

By owning both asset styles A and B you can smooth out the return as shown in the combined A and B chart. Both end up at the same place, but the volatility or risk is greatly reduced by owning them together. In actual practice, owning different types of assets or styles of stocks would not give an investor a perfectly smooth investment return as shown in the combined A and B chart, but overall it would tend to smooth out or minimize volatility over time. Lower volatility means less dramatic downward periods which, in laymen's terms, allows you to sleep better.

As an example, from the charts of large cap versus small cap, you can see the same principles work for growth and value and for international and domestic. It is possible to own together big-cap funds, small- and mid-cap funds, domestic and international funds, growth funds, and value funds. Owning such a diversified group of investments should decrease volatility.

PROTECTING LARGE INVESTMENT AMOUNTS FROM RISK

There are statistical models, based on historical performance that optimize a person's portfolio by maximizing return for various levels of risk, called the Efficient Frontier. This optimization by asset type (stocks, bonds, CDs, treasury bills, real estate, etc.) and style diversification (growth and value, big and small, domestic and international) minimizes volatility or downward risk without sacrificing much total return. The larger the portfolio, the less time you have before taking funds out, and the lower your willingness to take risk, the more significant it is to protect your funds by the use of asset allocation.

For the 20 years ending September 30, 1999, it would have been possible to capture 85% of the all-stock return with 35% less volatility with 60% invested in a large-cap stock fund and 40% invested in an intermediate bond portfolio. This is a very simple asset allocation and yet accomplishes most of what a more sophisticated asset allocation can do.

Asset allocation and lower risk are good. However, lowering risk usually involves giving up something in return, quite literally. Additionally, given enough time, the up-and-down movement of volatility does not hurt long-term results unless you are forced to sell out prematurely. If you invest for the long haul, you can wait out volatility. Invest early in a well-diversified stock portfolio. As the portfolio becomes sizeable, and as you get closer to the time of withdrawal, use asset allocation to protect against volatility.

VIII

KEEPING COSTS DOWN AND INDEX FUNDS

FINDING TOP-PERFORMING FUNDS

FOR this strategy of growing $2,000 into $1,000,000 to work optimally, an investor has to capture a 12% return, approximately the average return of the stock market for the last 75-plus years. Average is just what it implies; there are better returns and worse returns, but 12% is the average. The main consideration for us is how to ensure that you perform at the average or better.

Average performance does not take into consideration costs associated with a mutual fund: transaction costs, which are the costs to buy or sell a stock within the fund, and management fees, which are what the company that manages the fund charges for their services. These expenses, depending on the amount of the costs and the performance of your fund, could push your results below average.

There are two ways to address this concern. One way is to buy a well-diversified mutual fund in which the performance exceeds the average in an amount that equals or exceeds the costs associated with that fund. This is not as easy as it sounds, but it is possible. A number of services rank mutual funds. One of them, Morningstar, found in most libraries, ranks funds from 5 to 1 with 5 being the highest performance rating, taking into account both return and risk. Morningstar ratings are weighted on longer-term performance of several years, which is more significant than short-term performance of a year or less. The top-rated funds over an extended period are the funds most likely to continue to outperform. However, that can change, particularly if the manager responsible for the performance leaves the firm, or if a particular style goes into an extended period of underperformance. With a well-diversified fund, the chance of the latter happening is more remote.

To help select a fund, I suggest you pick a well-diversified fund recommended highly by Morningstar or that you set up an appointment with your local banker or broker for advice. If you are a minor, you may want to go with a parent if they have a bank or brokerage relationship and if you would feel more comfortable with them there. I know I would be pleased to visit with a young adult and answer questions, and I think most other bankers and brokers would, too.

BUYING AN INDEX FUND

The other way to address the concern of ensuring that your portfolio performance is equal to the averages is to try to greatly minimize costs rather than try to exceed the averages. One way to do this is by buying low-cost index funds. An index fund is a fund that replicates a widely followed group of stocks that is representative of the overall stock market. The most widely followed index is the Standard and Poor 500, or S&P 500, for short, which represents the performance of the 500 largest companies based on market capitalization traded on national stock exchanges. This index amounts to approximately 75% of the total market value of all stocks traded. This is also a legitimate approach to implementing our strategy.

There are a number of reasons why buying an index fund is a reasonable approach. First, by buying index funds, you are diversifying among 500 to 5,000 stocks, simultaneously diversifying among styles. Owning common index funds can give you big and small capitalization diversification, and also growth and value style diversification. Although this does not give an investor an international fund, most large domestic companies have such international exposure that they rather effectively allow an investor to participate in international markets without owning international funds.

As I stated before, the S&P 500 is weighted heavily (capitalization weighted) to the largest stocks. This means the better the largest stocks do, the better the index does. Alternately, the Wilshire 5000, despite its name, has an equal weighting among approximately 7,000 U.S. stocks. As a result of the weighting of the S&P 500, the Wilshire 5000 (in conjunction with the S&P 500) may help you be more fully diversified among large and small caps. A better solution than owning both—or one or the other—is to own a total market fund that duplicates both. Vanguard and T. Rowe Price both have these funds, which get most of the return of the S&P 500 but also capture the performance of small stocks. The minimum investment is as low as $1,000. Again, a broker or banker can help you with this. Alternately, many funds now allow you to get information online and deal with them directly.

Costs of Mutual Funds Vs. Index Funds

The second reason to consider the purchase of index funds is cost. The argument for this is that costs can cause a significant difference, especially for the long-term investor. As I have shown previously, stocks have had an approximate 12% long-term compound growth rate. That growth rate is without the cost of owning the fund. The average mutual fund has an expense ratio of 1.4%–1.5% (the expenses charged by the managers of the fund).

Additionally, the average equity mutual fund turns over 85%–90% per year. This means that if there were 100 stocks in a portfolio, 85 to 90 on average would be sold at some time during the year. That turnover costs the fund another .5%–1.5% per year. These two costs will aggregate on average between 2%–2.5%.

Additionally, the high turnover in an average mutual fund compared to the low turnover in an index fund can create a 2% differential in performance in a taxable account over a 20-year period. This differential is a result of paying taxes sooner with heavy turnover as opposed to deferring them longer with very little turnover. Money not spent in taxes can compound. That makes a large difference. Chart 8.1 shows these costs and the difference costs can make.

	INDEX FUNDS	STOCK MUTUAL FUND—TAXABLE	STOCK MUTUAL FUND—TAX SHELTERED
Average Return	12.00%	12.00%	12.00%
Performance			
Management	(.25%–.50%)	(1.50%)	(1.50%)
Fees			
Transaction Costs		(1.00%)	(1.00%)
Tax Inefficiency (or Acceleration of Tax)		(2.00%)	
Actual Return	11.50%–11.75%	7.50%	9.50%

CHART 8.1

Adding up all of the above means that an average-cost mutual fund that performs only average in a fully taxable fund (no tax shelters like the Roth IRA) would return, after fees, not 12% but approximately 7.5% (column 2). In a tax-sheltered account like a Roth IRA, traditional IRA, or education IRA, the net return for an average stock mutual fund would be approximately 9.5% (column 3). An index fund (column 1) will perform average by definition. That is what it is designed to do—replicate an average. But it has a very low cost structure, so the costs run only .25%–.50% annually, resulting in an 11.50%–11.75% return.

Which Is Best: Index Fund or Top Performer?

Is it possible to offset these fees and costs in a mutual fund with outstanding portfolio management? Yes, it probably is, but remember that a 12% stock return is average. The argument for the proponents of indexing is this: Average means that half the stock managers will perform worse than average and half will perform better—before costs. Factoring in a 2.5% or more performance disadvantage from costs significantly lowers the chances that a mutual fund will outperform the market over the long-term. Although performance varies by style and time frame, most studies show fewer than 20% of the managers outperform the index over an extended period.

According to *Money*[13] magazine in 1998, the S&P 500 index outperformed 80% of all general equity funds. The year before it was 95%, and the year before that it was 75%. Since 1972 and ending in 1998, there have been nine years when more than half the nation's general funds outperformed the S&P index and 17 years in which they haven't. In the 12 years ending in 1998, the average annual return via an index was 15% versus 14.2% in a typical equity fund.

In one study, Ira Weiss, an accounting professor at Columbia Business School, found that diversified U.S. stock funds gained 10.2% over a 36-year period ending in December 1997, compared to 11.6% for the S&P 500 index. Even small differences in costs can make a significant

[13] "The Age of Indexing in 1998," *Money*, April 1999.

impact. One hundred thousand dollars invested for 20 years at 12% would accumulate to $19,000 more with an annual expense difference of just one-tenth of 1% per year.

Some evidence does seem to show that highly touted funds have not outperformed the averages. Additionally, some studies have tried to show that services such as Morningstar and the Forbes Honor Roll Funds have not generated market-beating returns. According to one of these studies, in the 25 years ending June 1998, the Forbes Honor Roll Funds were up 13.6% per year versus 14.3% for the S&P 500.

Although it may be possible to pick a fund whose manager can consistently outperform the index by an amount greater than the costs associated with an actively managed fund, proponents of indexing say that the odds are substantially against it. Jonathan Clements, the personal finance columnist for *The Wall Street Journal* and a convert to index funds, says, "The logic of costs is irrefutable. You can't change the math."

A well-diversified mutual fund with a long-term track record of exceeding the averages by an amount that exceeds the fund's costs is one way to help ensure that performance equals the long-term growth rate of stocks. Again, be conscious of costs, because low costs give the manager a better chance of outperformance. Ask your broker or banker for help. Alternately, a low-risk way to replicate average performance at a low cost is to use index funds for the reasons described above. Either approach will work. It is a matter of personal choice. If you are not sure, you may want to ask a reputable finance advisor, broker, or banker for his or her advice.

There have been a number of times after writing the first edition of this book that I have been asked to recommend a particular fund. There are many good funds available, as discussed above, and your broker, banker, financial advisor, or services like Morningstar can give you information in this area. Saying that, following is an example of a fund I like and reasons I like it.

My recommended fund is American Centuries Washington Mutual (I have bought some of this fund for my own kids). I like it because it has an excellent long-term track record dating back to 1952. Additionally, it has low annual costs of .65% (remember, average fund costs are 1.5%) and low turnover (remember, high turnover can mean higher transaction costs). Finally, it is conservatively managed, purchasing quality stocks, and therefore historically has had lower risk or volatility than the overall market—all of which I like.

I should also note that when you buy a fund through a broker, typically there is a load or one-time sales cost of 4%–7% of the purchase price. The fund mentioned above has a 5.75% load through a broker. However, you can purchase Class B shares that have no load but a higher annual fee. Either way works out about the same. If you buy a fund with a load, I would suggest paying for this one-time fee with extra funds so that you do not subtract from your initial investment ($2,000 or whatever the amount). As an example, 5.75% of $2,000 = $115. Although this is 5.75% of your initial investment, it is small relative to the ultimate long-term growth potential ($1 million or more).

IX

SPENDING LESS THAN YOU EARN

MY OWN RULES

WHEN I began working at the bank as a trainee in 1974, my annual salary was $10,800. That may not seem like a huge amount now, but at the time it really was a very good starting salary. I was starting work right out of college, was single, and had no debt and some savings. I was fortunate to not have any school debt. I went to a moderate-sized public school, Northwest Missouri State University, located 40 miles from my hometown. College was not that expensive at the time, only $1,100 per year for tuition, room, and board. With a tennis scholarship and an academic scholarship and working as a resident hall director, I was able to pay about 75% of the costs, and my parents paid the rest. In my first few years of work following school, I rented an apartment, fully furnished, for $85 per month. My landlord said I could stay there as long as I wanted at that same rent. (If I had only taken him up on that.) Being single, it was particularly easy to control my expenses. I had a 1964

Buick LeSabre, a 10-year-old car that still ran well. I really didn't need much extra. I did buy a new television in the first few months, but other than that I was pretty well set. At that time, I set up several rules for myself. They were as follows:

1. I saved something out of every paycheck.

2. Anything I bought during the year, I bought out of the current year's savings so that I still saved some money by the end of the year. This required some discipline, particularly when I replaced cars periodically. But it really forced me to save during the year and to not overspend on a car.

3. I paid all my taxes, including investment earnings, out of current earnings.This was easy, at first, but became tougher in later years as taxes on accumulated investments became larger. This again put a discipline on me that kept my investments growing without being penalized by tax reduction. Also, it helped that I continued to advance in the company and my earnings increased each year.

These three personal rules served me well, especially when I was first starting out. Now, almost 30 years later, I am not nearly as stringent on my rules as I was in the first 20–25 years, but I don't need to be.

Budgeting

This book is not about budgeting, but budgeting is a big part of saving because you cannot save if you don't spend less than you earn. There are many people who make lots of money but spend more than they make. As a result, many end up in bankruptcy even though they have large earnings.

How you can start to control expenses is to monitor what you spend. Budgeting your monthly and annual expenses is a way of prioritizing, in advance, how you will spend your income. By laying out a plan, you can make choices on discretionary expenses.

Although this book is about the importance of saving and the power of compound interest, borrowing using credit cards can work against you in a dramatic way and will greatly diminish your ability to save and compound your funds. Some credit cards charge as high as 22.9% annual percentage yield. If you make the minimum payment required each month, which is interest and almost zero principal, you are in effect paying 22.9% annually for a very long time. One study showed that one $50 purchase at 22.9% interest, paying only the minimum payment each month, would total over $4,000 in payments in 20 years.[14] If 22.9% is allowed to compound, using The Rule of 72, you can see how that money would double in a little over three years ($72 \div 22.9 = 3.14$). That can restrict your ability to save and compound your savings tremendously. Here is a good rule for credit cards. Never use them unless you can and will pay the bill in full when your bill comes the next month. If you do this, you will never pay high credit card interest. If you can't use this discipline, don't use credit cards at all.

---

[14] Dara Duguay, *Please Send Money: A financial Survival Guide for Young Adults on Their Own.* Sourcebooks, Inc., Naperville, Il., 2001.

Once you have laid out all your expenses, it can be helpful to see how your expenses compare against what others spend. Here are some statistics broken down by the percentage spent in each major category of a budget.

Typically, mortgage or rent payments, usually one of the biggest items in a budget, total 20%–30% of take-home or after-tax pay. Utilities run 4%–7%. Food, the second biggest item, takes 15%–20%, followed by transportation, which can run between 6%–20%. Other personal expenses run between 5%–10%.[15]

Normally, you should set aside 2%–8% of pay for less frequent bills such as clothing and medical expenses. It is important to keep loan payments other than a mortgage between 10%–20% of income—lower is better.

SAMPLE BUDGET	
	RANGE OF TAKE-HOME PAY
House Payment or Rent	20% – 30%
Food	15% – 20%
Transportation	6% – 20%
Utilities	4% – 7%
Personal Expenses	5% – 10%
Less Frequent Bills (clothing, medicine, etc.)	2% – 8%
Savings	5% – 20%
Giving	3% – 10%

CHART 9.1

---

[15] Gene Meyer, "Getting Your Budget on Track," *Kansas City Star*, March 29,1998

Bankers like me prefer to see total loan payments (house payment, all installment payments for cars, etc., and credit card payments) at 40% or less of gross income (pretax). In fact, it is very difficult to get a loan if payments exceed this percentage. As an example, if a couple's pretax income is $36,000 per year, or $3,000 per month, their total monthly loan payments should be less than $1,200 ($3,000 x 40% = $1,200). Normally, anything higher is potentially asking for trouble.

Saving in "Buckets"

Many people advise that you save in three "buckets." The first bucket, for emergencies, contingencies, or unexpected events, might be 5% of your annual income. Many financial planners suggest 3 to 6 months of annual income in a ready cash reserve for contingencies and emergencies.

For an adult, saving this contingency fund is probably a good idea before saving and investing for other goals and needs, including long-term saving. For a student or young adult, the answer may depend on your family situation. If your parents will most likely help you through emergencies, I believe it is fine to begin saving for the long-term now. On the other hand, if as a student or young adult you will have to handle emergencies yourself, like your car breaking down, it may be advisable to save for both at the same time. This may also encourage you to save more. Keep in mind that in most cases the long-term savings can be accessed in a dire situation without substantial negative consequences.

The second bucket is for short- and intermediate-term goals: a car, a house, education, vacation, or many other items. This might also be 5% of your income. The third bucket is for long-term savings that you plan not to touch. Ideally, this could be 5%–10% also, but 10% would be best. This is the money you want to have to retire on, and much or all of it can be saved in tax-sheltered investments. Also, as this pool of funds accumulates sufficiently, you can draw from the annual interest for needs other than retirement and still have the principal continue to grow. (This is discussed in the chapter entitled "When Do I Enjoy It?")

SETTING GOALS

Budgeting is about prioritizing resources toward your most important goals and needs. An important part of this is determining your goals and then determining a plan to reach them. Research shows that the best way to accomplish a goal is to write it down. If you don't write it down, it is only a thought, an idea, or a dream.

Every year, I personally write down my goals for the year, financial and otherwise. Then I devise plans to reach them. Finally, I refer to them frequently to see how I am doing. What is written down is much more likely to get accomplished. It is equally important to write down financial goals and create plans to reach those goals. That is where a budget comes into play.

My wife, Marla, taught school for four years, two years while we were dating and two years after we were married and before we had our first child. Before we were married, she used a system of putting money from her paycheck into envelopes for food, clothes, etc. The money in each envelope was all she planned to spend in that category. When it was gone, it was gone. This was a method of providing herself budgeting discipline, and it worked for her. Unfortunately, she does not do this now, and therefore her expenses are higher. (Hopefully she won't read this part of my book.)

MAJOR PURCHASES AND THEIR EFFECTS ON SAVINGS

The largest single purchase most people make is their home. Is it best that you not buy a home? Generally, the answer is no. Typically, a home not only holds its value but increases in value over time. According to *Forbes*[16] magazine, the long-term, real, inflation-adjusted rate of home values in the United States averages 0.3%. With the long-term inflation rate at approximately 3%, that means home values should increase on a nominal basis at approximately 3.3%. Hence, with normal upkeep, a house can be expected to go up in value. Therefore, it is a type of savings. Obviously, it is important not to buy a home that is more than you can afford either in payments or upkeep. But if it is maintained, a home will generally increase in value.

The second largest purchase made by most people is a car. For young adults, it is the largest. After a home and

---

[16] Stephan Fitch, "Did You Pay Too Much?" *Forbes*, October 18, 1999.

car, single-item purchases drop significantly in size. Yes, food costs a lot, but we have to eat. Likewise, food is not a single item. It is a series of daily expenses. Clothing is also expensive, but no single piece of clothing costs anywhere near as much as a car. A car is generally an essential need. It must be reliable and safe. The problem is that over time, cars decrease in value, unlike a house. A vehicle is the single largest expense you have that consistently goes down in value. In fact, a $20,000 new car may drop in value up to $2,000 the day you drive it off the lot—because as of that day it is no longer new.

You need a car, so what are your choices? The main decision, usually, is how much you want to spend for reliable, safe transportation. Some people, particularly youth, spend a lot for status and style; they may buy a fancy new car as opposed to a reliable but less stylish car that is a few years old. Of course, it is their choice, but such a purchase can have long-term effects on potential savings.

Let's look at an example. Assume you can buy a $20,000 new car or a 4-year-old used car for $10,000. Let's assume that both are good, quality cars. Over the next five to seven years you can probably expect either car to provide you with reliable transportation. Let's assume that at the end of seven years both cars generally will be worth very little. The newer car may be worth slightly more at that time. Also, the newer car probably costs less for repairs and maintenance.

But the newer car also costs more in insurance, particularly for young adults under 25. With a used car you may be able to purchase liability insurance only. Liability insurance means you are covered only for damage you cause to others as required by law, not for damage to your own car. The lower the value of your car, the more financial sense it makes to carry liability coverage only. If you buy a new car costing $20,000, you will want full coverage which, in addition to liability insurance, covers your car for damage that was your fault, costing an estimated additional $400 every six months, assuming you are under age 25 and single. The higher the value of the car, the more important it is to have full coverage to protect you from loss should you be at fault in damage to your own car. The difference in insurance of $400 every six months or $800 per year is sizeable. Insurance is especially expensive for young drivers, because they are the least experienced and, therefore, have the most accidents and claims. Personal property tax and sales tax will also be higher on the new car.

Without attempting to analyze each item of these expenses, my premise is that both cars provide reliable transportation— one at a $10,000 higher initial cost. The real tradeoff for that cost was style and status.

Most people pay for a car by making monthly payments for three, four, or five years. In that case, the actual difference is larger because you are making payments with interest, additional money that could have been saved. Unfortunately, in my banking experience, I've seen a number of people who have never saved money continue to pay for new cars on an installment basis nearly their entire lives. In these cases, the lost potential for wealth accumulation given modest savings and investing, time, and compounding is enormous. As an example, an extra $10,000 financed on a car at 12% over 48 months would cost $263 per month for a total of $12,640; of that, $2,640 is interest.

If you choose to spend $10,000 for a nicer car, that is not the end of the world. But consider that discretionary expense in terms of The Rule of 72. Let's say a 20-year-old has a choice to spend $10,000 extra on a nicer car or save the difference in a lump sum. If the extra money described above used to finance a $10,000 fancier car were instead saved and invested at 12%, this would accumulate to $16,101 after 48 months at age 24.[17] Then, using The Rule of 72, it could have grown to approximately $32,000 by age 30, $64,000 by age 36, $128,000 by age 42, $256,000 by age 48, $512,000 by age 54, and $1,024,000 by age 60.

Large discretionary expenses need to be considered in terms of not only the initial cost differential but in terms of the lost accumulation potential. Ten thousand dollars may not seem like that big of a loss today, especially because you get something for it—like a brand new car. But at age 60, $1,000,000 is a very large loss. I like vehicles as much as the next person, and it is enjoyable to have a new one, but consider the real tradeoff not only in today's dollars but

---

[17] Saving $263 each month for 48 months at 12% grows to $16,101. Total loan payments of $263 for 48 months amounts to only $12,640. The reason for the difference is that the loan payment reduces principal each month, so that 12% is accruing on a smaller amount each month. Contrast that with $263 saved each month at 12% where the saved amount and accumulated interest keeps growing. Then 12% accumulates on a larger figure each month.

in future growth and compounding potential. This discussion can relate to any large discretionary expense, not just cars. If you do decide to wait and save the difference, there may still be a good time to buy a new car, potentially a much nicer one than you might buy now. When your money has grown significantly and it is working for you, take some of the growth or interest to buy a new car.

A lady in our banking company purchased the first printing of this book for her daughter. After her daughter, then 17, finished reading the book, her mother told me that her daughter had decided against buying the new car she had been saving for. Instead, she planned to invest the money as described in this book. If she gives this savings time to grow, someday she will be able to buy a nicer car from one year's interest! More on this subject in Chapter 12.

"I wonder where these car payments will lead me?"

X

THE ROTH INDIVIDUAL RETIREMENT ACCOUNT

THE TRADITIONAL IRA

BEFORE we get into the details of the Roth IRA, let's look at the traditional IRA, or Individual Retirement Account, which has been around for a number of years. Through year-end 2001, it allowed individuals who do not participate in a qualified retirement account (and individuals within certain income limits who do participate in a qualified retirement account) to make tax-deductible contributions of up to $2,000 annually. The Economic Growth and Tax Relief Reconciliation Act of 2001 raised the IRA limits to $3,000 in 2002, increasing to $4,000 in 2005, and $5,000 in 2008, after which time it is indexed with inflation in $500 increments. In addition, the money grows tax-deferred until it is withdrawn at retirement or any time after the year in which a person reaches age 59$\frac{1}{2}$.

As an example, since contributions to a traditional IRA are tax deductible, a person who is in a 32% income tax bracket

QUESTION	TRADITIONAL IRA	ROTH IRA
Are there income limits on the ability to make nonde-ductible contributions?	No.	Yes. The phaseouts are $95,000 to $110,000 AGI for single filers and $150,000 to $160,000 AGI for joint filers.
Is there an annual contribu-tion limit?	Yes, $3000* per person to all IRAs combined.	Yes, $3,000* per person to all IRAs combined.
Are contributions deductible?	Yes, for nonparticipants in an employer plan. For others, the 2002 phaseouts are $34,000 to $44,000 AGI for single fil-ers and $54,000 to $64,000 AGI for joint filers.	No, all contributions are nondeductible, after-tax contributions.
Can a non-income-earning spouse contribute to an IRA?	Yes, up to $3,000* per person to all IRAs combined, provided there is an income-earning spouse. No, if neither spouse earns income.	Yes, up to $3,000* per person to all IRAs combined, provided there is an income-earning spouse. No, if neither spouse earns income.
Can a spouse who is not a participant in an employer plan make fully deductible IRA contributions?	Yes. The phaseout range is $150,000 to $160,000 AGI on a joint return.	No. All contributions are nondeductible.
Are earnings tax deferred?	Yes.	Yes.
How are withdrawals taxed after age 59 1/2?	Withdrawals are subject to tax. Exception: pro rata share of nondeductible contributions.	Withdrawals are tax free if account held 5 years. Contributions are withdrawn tax free at any time.
Must withdrawals begin at age 70 1/2?	Yes.	No.
Are contributions allowable after age 70 1/2?	No.	Yes, if owner has earned income.
How are withdrawals taxed before age 59 1/2?	Withdrawals are subject to tax. A 10% penalty is added except in the case of: • death, • disability, • life annuity, • "first" home purchase (up to $10,000), • educational expenses, • medical expenses, or • health insurance for unemployed.	Contributions are withdrawn tax free. Withdrawals of earnings from accounts held 5 years are tax free in the case of: • death, • disabiltiy, or • "first " home purchase (up to $10,000). Withdrawals of earnings are subject to tax but no penalty in the case of: • life annuity, • educational expenses, • medical expenses, or • health insurance for unemployed. All other withdrawals of earnings are subject to tax plus 10% penalty.
What rules apply to rollovers from a traditional IRA to a Roth IRA?		Investor's income must be under $100,000. The roll-over is taxed, but the 10% penalty does not apply.

*May be increased by $500 for individuals age 50 or over.

(combined federal and state) would save 32% of every dollar contributed to the IRA. Remember Wesley from Chapter 6? Therefore, if a person made a $2,000 contribution, he or she would save $640 in income taxes. Additionally, earnings on the IRA are tax-deferred, which means there is no tax on earnings until the money is withdrawn. So If a person set up an IRA and purchased a stock fund in the IRA that earns 12% compounded, the money will compound without any tax consequences until withdrawal. Because of the tax deduction now, and the tax deferral of interest, the IRS does tax the IRA at the time of withdrawal—which must begin no later than the year the investor reaches 70½.

> Wouldn't it be great to have no tax on money as it is earned and no tax on the interest as it grows (combining the features of the traditional IRA and the Roth IRA)?
>
> A Roth IRA for students combines the best of both worlds.

Contrast owning a stock fund within an IRA with owning a stock fund that earns 12% that is not tax shel-tered, which we call a taxable account. As the stock fund in a taxable account earns 12%, there will be taxes on the income. The taxes actual-ly paid depend on when the stocks within the fund are sold and whether they are long-term or short-term gains or loss-es. For simplicity's sake, let's assume the 12% generates short-term capital gains. As a result, the investor will pay income tax at 32% of the 12% gain. If you subtract the taxes from the 12% gain, you will have left only 8.16%, which will not grow as fast as 12%.

Although, as mentioned above, taxes on an IRA are paid at withdrawal, the IRA account has had time to earn

	Taxable Investment $1,360 at 8.16%	Traditional IRA $2,000 at 12%	Roth IRA $1,360 at 12%	Student* Roth IRA $2,000 at 12%
THE STUDENT ROTH IRA				
Years				
10	$2,979	$6,211	$4,223	$6,211
20	$6,529	$19,292	$13,118	$19,292
30	$14,306	$59,919	$40,745	$59,918
40	$31,347	$185,101	$126,549	$186,101
50	$68,686	$578,004	$393,042	$578,004
54.83	$100,326	$1,000,000	$680,000	$1,000,000
		($320,000) tax = $680,000		

CHART 10.2

*The Student Roth IRA is not an official name. It is a name I use to describe the combination of benefits that a student gets assuming the student has no taxable income.

money on money that would have gone to the government—both the tax deduction that saved you money when you made the contribution and the part of the earnings that would have also gone to taxes each year.

Let's look at an example, shown in Chart 10.2, of how much difference this can make. Without the tax deduction in the IRA, $2,000 allows only $1,360 to be invested ($2,000 x 32% tax rate = $640 tax). Additionally, annual taxes on earnings, such as might occur in the typical mutual fund, lowers the overall return significantly. A 12% return becomes an 8.16% return based on a combined federal and state tax rate of 32%. At the end of 54.83 years, the traditional IRA is worth $1,000,000 and the taxable investment is worth $100,326. To actually make an apples-to-apples comparison, it should be noted that when the IRA is withdrawn it would be taxed, whereas the taxable investment has already been taxed. Therefore, when the million dollars is withdrawn from the IRA it becomes $680,000 after taxes. In practice, the money would be drawn out over an extended period of time, but this serves to show the difference—$680,000 compared to a little over $100,000, almost a 7-fold difference.

THE ROTH IRA

The Roth IRA in the fourth column of Chart 10.2 is a new vehicle that does not provide an initial tax deduction, but it does provide tax-free (not tax-deferred) earnings. Some of the rules are the same, like the contribution limits described previously. By giving up the initial deduction, the IRS allows the interest to grow tax-free. How does this compare to a traditional, tax-deductible IRA? Well, the numbers work out exactly the same. After 54.83 years, you have $680,000 with the tax already paid. After you pay tax on the regular IRA, you also have $680,000.

> If a 15-year-old saved $2,000 per year for 10 years, what would it be worth in 54 years?
>
> Answer: $5,645,725

Wouldn't it be great to have the tax deduction upfront and tax-free growth all in one? Yes, it would, and it can be done. Here is how: Since the Roth rules allow all earned income up to $3,000 annually in 2002 to be contributed into this account, a teenager who earned $2,000[18] or more could contribute all of that $2,000 into the Roth, which we know

[18] If a student earns less than $2,000, the concepts described above will still work but can take a little longer, or you can start a little earlier. As an example, $500 earned and saved each summer will take four summers to reach $2,000. So don't be discouraged if you don't earn $2,000 all in one year.

would grow tax-free. He or she should have no tax with that income based on a standard deduction of $4,700 for the tax year 2002. That means there is no tax on the first $4,700 of earned income. Therefore, it is virtually tax-deductible and tax-free. As a result, we can combine our charts so that the $2,000 grows tax-free to $1,000,000 in 54.83 years—having your cake and eating it too (see the fifth column on Chart 10.2). It should be noted that assets owned by a child can potentially decrease the likelihood of receiving as much college assistance from grants and financial aid. Colleges require parents and the student to fill out forms requesting financial aid. Approximately 5% of assets in the parents' name are expected to be used toward college, whereas 35% of assets in the child's name are expected to be used. Custodial accounts are actually owned by the child and, therefore, could be more detrimental to receiving financial aid than the parent owning the asset themselves. Although the Roth is in the child's name, most colleges do not consider the Roth as being available for college; hence, there is no detrimental effect on the aid formulas by owning a Roth. In addition to the asset ownership affecting financial aid, student income can also have an effect.

Currently as of 2002, the magic numbers for income that can be earned by a student in one year without an effect on aid is $2,247 (this is another reason why $2,000 earned and saved in a Roth works so well). For every $1.00 earned above $2,247, fifty cents is counted against financial aid eligibility. If you do earn more than $2,247 and you put it into a Roth, the penalty for financial aid eligibility is 35 cents of every dollar rather than 50 cents—so the Roth helps in this situation also.

An obvious question for a parent would be: do you really think my 15-year-old son or daughter is going to put all $2,000 of his or her summer income into a Roth IRA? Probably not. So why don't you put some of it in for your child, or have him or her read this book and match your child's contribution, or even pay it all.

There is no tax on any gift up to $11,000 per donor, per recipient, so give your child or children $2,000 each, or better yet have their grandparents give it to them. If the child can resist withdrawing it, he or she will be very glad someday that you did this.

What if you contribute $2,000 per year for your child between the ages of 15 and 25 as he or she earns $2,000 per summer? At the end of 54.83 years, assuming 12% per year, the Roth IRA would be worth $5,645,725. Not a bad result for ten $2,000 gifts.

RULES FOR THE ROTH IRA

Here are the important pieces of information you should know concerning the Roth IRA:

- All earned income can be contributed, up to $3,000 in 2002 (perfect for a student with part-time employment).

- Full eligibility is limited to individual taxpayers with modified adjusted gross income less than $95,000, with phased-down eligibility to modified adjusted gross income up to $110,000; and full eligibility for couples filing jointly with modified adjusted gross income less than $150,000, with phased-down eligibility up to modified adjusted gross income of $160,000 (in year 2002).

- A qualified distribution is exempt from taxes and penalties. There are requirements to be "qualified."

    Requirement #1—The Roth IRA must have been in existence five years beginning with the first taxable year for which the holder made a contribution.

    Requirement #2—The distribution must occur after one of the following events: attainment of age $59\frac{1}{2}$, disability, the purchase of a first home, or death.

- Withdrawals that are not qualified are withdrawn from principal contributions first. There is no tax or penalty on principal contribution withdrawals.

- After principal is completely withdrawn, additional withdrawals from interest or earnings are taxed as regular income. In addition, the interest or earnings amount is subject to a 10% penalty unless one of the following events has occurred: reaching age $59\frac{1}{2}$ —or older, death, disability, setting up withdrawals on substantial equal periodic payments, health insurance, medical expenses, education expenses, or buying a first home. The substantial equal payments are a very reasonable approach to the withdrawal for substantial accumulation prior to reaching age $59\frac{1}{2}$.

These restrictions are less severe than with traditional IRAs. With the Roth you can always withdraw the principal without penalty and, in many situations of need as described above, you can withdraw the interest without tax and penalties. Again, it should be noted that except as described above, the interest could be subject to tax and penalty prior to age 59½. But remember, the idea is to keep it in and give it time to grow rather than withdrawing it early. Also, Roth IRAs can be deferred for an entire lifetime, past age 70½, the starting distribution age of a traditional IRA.

Because there are restrictions on withdrawals, consider saving in a Roth IRA and, if possible, saving additional funds in a taxable investment. The Roth will grow the fastest and most efficiently based on the tax advantage. The other funds will also grow, but will be more readily available in case of emergency.

There is a way to extend the tax-free factor long past the death of the owner by naming a much younger beneficiary. A Roth IRA account holder can change his or her beneficiary designation at any time. Even if the account holder is over 70, he or she can make a change and name a younger beneficiary, such as a grandchild. The beneficiary is allowed to take distributions based on his or her own life expectancy.

As an example, assume you give your son $2,000 at age 15, and it grows to $1,000,000 by age 70. At that time, your son changes the beneficiary to his grandchild (your great-grandchild), who is 10 years old. At the death of the owner, the power of compounding is allowed to work potentially well over 100 years (estate taxes for the owner still apply for estates over $1,000,000 in 2002 and 2003, growing in subsequent years to $3,500,000 in 2009, unlimited in 2010, at which time it reverts back to $1,000,000 in 2011). This can be done only once. Your son's grandchild cannot name another beneficiary—such as his or her grandchild— to extend tax deferral further. The money has to be disbursed over the life expectancy of the named beneficiary.

The IRS has a Roth prototype agreement that can be used to sign up. Most all banks, brokerages, and other financial service providers have the standard Roth form.

"Okay, Number $2000, you run this play continuously until you make the $1,000,000 touchdown."

X I

S T R A T E G I E S

START WITH EARNED INCOME—
SAVE INTO THE ROTH

BASED on the principles we have discussed, what are the best strategies to maximize these results? Everyone has unique circumstances, so the strategies individuals use may be slightly different or even vastly different from each other.

For teenagers and other school-age young adults, try to find ways to earn enough so that you can save $2,000 or more in a Roth IRA. Remember that there are some restrictions on withdrawals that we have discussed previously, so you have to understand these restrictions and be prepared to let the funds grow and compound.

Depending on the circumstances, you may need to earn more than $2,000. For instance, if you are planning to pay for your higher education or if you have to earn money to pay for auto expenses, clothes, or extra spending money, you will need to earn funds for this plus money to contribute to the Roth IRA.

If you as a teenager or young adult cannot get a job that produces sufficient income to save and contribute to a Roth IRA, it may be possible for your parents to employ you. The rules on this are as follows: The IRS allows parents or grandparents to deduct reasonable wages paid to a minor child who works as their employee. The adult should make sure wages are reasonable with what they would pay a non-relative. Also, the parent or grandparent should take into account a child's age when setting the wage. Very young children can't reasonably do as much as older children. Further, the child must do business-related work. Household chores don't count. Finally, a child must be a true employee. The best way for a parent to show this is through the normal payroll process. If the business is incorporated, the owner will have to pay Social Security, Medicare, and unemployment taxes totaling 15.3%. If not incorporated, the parent may not have to contribute these taxes at all. Parents should check with their accountant.

If you earn some income but spend all or most of it, your parents can put an amount equal to your earnings in a Roth IRA for you. Your grandparents can do this instead if your parents are unable to do so. If the Roth restrictions for withdrawal are a major concern, invest in a taxable account with potentially lower tax, such as a lower turnover fund or an index fund.

For investments outside the Roth IRA, the Uniform Gift to Minors Act (UGMA) allows a parent or guardian to invest money in the child's account under the guardian's control until the minor reaches age 21. Although the child is the actual owner of record and is credited with what taxable earnings are created, he or she cannot withdraw the funds prior to age 21 without the guardian's written consent. A young adult should consider contributing to a Roth IRA as long as possible, and particularly as long as his or her taxable income is low enough that there is very little tax.

One way to help you save, particularly once you have a regular job, is to have your bank make an automatic withdrawal weekly or monthly into a savings or money market account. After it has accumulated sufficiently to invest in a stock fund, you can transfer it. Many stock funds and the index funds we have discussed allow very small additions once the initial amount (sometimes as low as $500) is met. This technique can also be used to transfer money from a parent's account into a child's account on a weekly or monthly basis. In order to encourage young adults to save, my banking company has an account that can be opened with as little as $10, and it is free from service charges. Once funds accumulate to $500, they can be transferred to a stock fund in our bank's brokerage department into either a taxable account or a Roth IRA, which provides for maximum growth.

Once you, the young adult, have a full-time job, maximize savings with regular savings deposits. Take advantage of tax shelters for at least a part of your savings, particularly that percentage with which you are comfortable allowing the funds to accumulate for the long-term. For long-term savings, take advantage of plans such as the tax-deductible traditional IRA, company sponsored 401(k) (particularly those with company matches) or profit sharing plans, and simple IRAs for self-employed and others.

Employer Retirement Accounts

When choosing an employer, consider very carefully the company benefits, including the retirement accounts, profit sharing, 401(k), and pension, and how much the company contributes on your behalf. These can be savings for you that do not come out of your pay. Most people underestimate the long-term value of good retirement benefits. In order to fully benefit, you may have to stay with the company until you are fully vested (the funds contributed by the employer are not really yours until you have met the appropriate length of service required). This can be up to five years without any vesting and then full vesting, or graduated vesting of up to a seven-year period. The principles of compounding and investing work the same as that which we have discussed but with potentially larger amounts since your employer is contributing to your account as well.

If you have the choice of investing in a 401(k) and if you are in for the long haul, invest more aggressively into equity funds based on the principles we have discussed.

It Is Not the Amount; it Is the Discipline and the Regularity.

The No. 1 strategy is to be disciplined! This entire concept is not a get-rich-quick scheme. Rather, it is a disciplined approach to long-term accumulation of wealth.

In my seminars, I emphasize to students that the really good and important things in life almost always require significant time and effort. Many people, unfortunately, avoid lofty goals because they are afraid of the effort, pain, or time they will require. I tell students that the easiest way to accomplish a large task or something of significance is to break it down into small pieces and then keep at it.

One of my hobbies is running marathons (my wife says I'm crazy). Twenty-six and two-tenths miles can seem overwhelming and impossible. But, it's not. First, I put in the training miles almost every day (regularly). Second, in the actual race, I break the race down into smaller and less overwhelming parts, one mile at a time, and at the end of the race even a step at a time. Finally, I have to keep going until I reach the end and accomplish the goal. Running a marathon or other significant goals or tasks are much easier when taken in smaller parts.

Saving to accumulate wealth is similar. It is not the amount that is important—it is the discipline and the regularity. To be wealthy, you don't need to start wealthy; you just need to start and stick with it. Start today and make it a lifelong discipline.

One final strategy for parents: One person who ordered my book wrote to tell me that his son had for many years been asking for a million dollars. The father wrote to tell me that he had decided to give his son this book instead. That is a good strategy, too!

Why not have your money work for you?

XII

ADDITIONAL STATEGIES
(FOR PARENTS AND GRANDPARENTS)

THE DR. FOSTER PLAN

ATTENDING one of my first seminars for high school students was Dr. Robert Foster, the president emeritus of Northwest Missouri State University in Maryville, my alma mater. Dr. Foster had been president of the university when I was in school—too many years ago to count. Subsequently, he was on one of our bank boards and is currently an advisory bank board member. He has helped me many times from college forward and is a very special person.

After the seminar, he told me that he wanted to use my concepts by contributing $2,000 to a Roth IRA for his new-born grandchild. I told him that this was not possible because a newborn would not have earned income, a requirement of the Roth. However, after I thought about this, I realized that he was on to something.

Although a newborn would not have earned income, a parent or grandparent can give their child or grandchild up to $11,000 per year without any gift tax consequences.[19] Therefore, a $2,000 gift would work fine. Normally, this is done using the Uniform Gift to Minors Act mentioned in the previous chapter, which allows an adult, usually a parent or grandparent, to be custodian for a minor's funds until they reach the age of majority, usually 18 or 21 in most states.

Assuming the gift from a parent or grandparent to a child or grandchild is $11,000 or less, there is no gift tax as mentioned above. Additionally, there is no income tax on the gift because it is not earned income or interest or dividends.

There is a provision in the tax law, known as the Kiddie Tax, which minimizes or eliminates tax below certain annual amounts. The rules are as follows: Your child (or grandchild) pays no tax on the first $750 of earned income such as interest or dividends or capital gains, and pays tax on the next $750 at his or her tax rate (with very little other income, it would be 10%). If the child receives more than $1,500 of earned income and is under age 14, he or she will be taxed at the parent or grandparent's tax rate (whoever is the custodian).

To summarize, for a $2,000 gift to a newborn, based on the Kiddie Tax mentioned above, there is a strong likelihood that there will be no income taxes for probably 15–20

---

[19] The $11,000 annual gift tax exclusion amount adjusts in $1,000 increments periodically based on inflation.

years. Hence, the money can grow tax-free for all practical purposes from birth until the time the child or grandchild has earned income. Then, it could be transferred into a Roth, probably for several more years worth of contributions. At that time, it will continue to grow tax-free for the child or grandchild's life and possibly longer, as described in the chapter about the Roth IRA.

Let's use some specifics. Let's assume a $2,000 gift to a grandchild is invested in a good quality stock fund that grows at 12% compounded annually. Using The Rule of 72, this amount would double every six years, so presumably you could expect it to be worth $4,000 at age 6, $8,000 at age 12, and $16,000 at age 18, all having occurred with very little, if any, tax, assuming no other earned income for the child or grandchild. At that time, let's assume that the child has earned income of $4,000 per year for the next several years. This money could then be transferred to a Roth IRA for, in this case, approximately four annual contributions.[20]

In effect, the whole concept in this book gets jumpstarted by 15–20 years. If a 15-year-old investing $2,000 had to wait until 69-plus to accumulate a million dollars, using this strategy, starting at birth allows a 15-year head start, which should provide a million dollar accumulation by age 54-plus! This, again, is with only one $2,000 gift. If the gift were larger or made annually, the results should be much

---

[20] Roth contribution limits increase substantially in future years. I have ignored additional growth on these funds for the four years for simplicity's sake. In actuality, the growth of the funds might grow for several more years of Roth contributions.

larger. Based on getting the idea for this from Dr. Foster, I call this the Dr. Foster Plan. Incidentally, Dr. Foster wrote a letter of instruction for the child and the child's parents indicating his desire that this money be allowed to grow and not be spent until it has accumulated sufficiently, unless it was needed for emergencies. Although this is not legally binding, it indicates his purpose and desire for the use of the funds.

STRATEGIES FOR EDUCATION EXPENSES

Another strategy for parents and grandparents saving for college involves the Coverdell Education IRA and the new 529 Plan, which began in 2002. The education IRA contribution limit quadrupled in 2002 to $2,000.[21] There is no deduction for a contribution, but it grows tax-free even at withdrawal as long as it is used for the cost of education from kindergarten through college, not just college. If the funds are not used by age 30, the account transfers to the child.

The new 529 Plan also grows tax-free (again, no deduction for contributions) as long as funds are withdrawn for higher education. The maximum yearly contribution is $55,000 per donor for each donee, usually a child or grandchild, or $110,000 per couple for each donee, again usually a child or grandchild. If the maximum is reached, this counts for five years of gifting to the recipient. Some states allow contributions up to $250,000, but this would exceed the annual gift tax limitations, which may still be advisable in

---

[21] The ability to make contributions is phased out for individuals with income between $95,000 and $110,000 and for couples with income between $190,000 and $225,000.

some cases. See your accountant for specifics as they relate to your particular circumstances.

The 529 Plan is a terrific way for parents to sock away large sums that can grow tax-free. Let's assume a parent has a choice of saving $10,000 for a newborn's college expenses or putting $10,000 into a 529 Plan. What difference could that make? Using The Rule of 72, let's examine that question. If $10,000 grew at 12% tax-free, it would double every six years. Therefore, it would be worth $20,000 at age 6, $40,000 at age 12, and $80,000 at age 18. Alternately, if the 12% earned is taxed, let's assume it earns only 8% after taxes, which would be 33% for taxes. Eight percent would double every nine years, which would mean the $10,000 would be worth $20,000 at age 9 and $40,000 at age 18. You can see that the same $10,000 would be worth twice as much in 18 years because of this tax-free feature!

> Using The Rule of 72, $10,000 growing at 12% tax free in a 529 Plan could grow to $80,000 in 18 years. Alternatively, $10,000 in a taxable account growing at 12% before taxes (but 8% after taxes) grows to $40,000 in 18 years.

Additionally, many states offer a state income tax deduction for contributions up to a maximum of usually $10,000 to their state-sponsored programs. These programs also provide funds with very low annual costs and no loads, both important additional benefits. There is a 10% penalty for non-qualified withdrawals.

Education expense is obviously a big concern for most everyone with children. The average annual cost for public

Type of Account	Income Limits	Contribution Limits	Contribution Deadline	Time Limits on Withdrawals	Ability to Change Beneficiary
529 Plans (General)	None	Max: Varies by state: Some allow balance limits as high as $305,000/beneficiary. Min: Varies by state. Annual: In the 1st year may contribute 5x the current annual gift tax exclusion amount w/o exceeding the annual federal gift tax exclusion	None	Varies by state	Yes (to avoid tax penalty, must be a member of the previous beneficiary's family)
Coverdell Education Savings Account	Joint: $190,000-$220,000 Single: $95,000-$110,000	Max: $2000/beneficiary Min: Varies by Investment Company	As late as April 15th of the following year	Funds must be used prior to beneficiary reaching age 30, or transferred to another family member, or distributed to the beneficiary as a non-qualified distribution.	Yes (to avoid tax penalty, must be a member of the previous beneficiary's family)

Owner of Assets/ Income	Control of Withdrawals	Investment Options	Contributions Deductibility	Qualified Use of Proceeds	Taxation of Qualified Withdrawals
Assets: Account Owner Income: Beneficiary	Account Owner	Varies by state	Federal: None State: Varies by state	Any accredited undergraduate/ graduate school expenses, such as tuition, books, and room and board.	Tax Free
Student	Account Guardian	Wide range of securities	Federal: None State: None	Primary, Secondary, & Higher Education (tuition, fees, tutoring, books, room and board, transportation, and equipment) (includes: computer peripheral equipment, software, and Internet access).	Tax Free

PENALTIES/TAXATION NON-QUALIFIED WITHDRAWALS	WITHDRAWALS DUE TO DEATH, DISABILITY, SCHOLARSHIP:	ROLLOVER	HOPE/LIFETIME LEARNING CREDIT
Earnings taxed at owner's rate plus a 10% penalty. If you deducted your contribution on a state income tax return, you will need to report additional state "recapture" income.	Not subject to Non-qualified Withdrawal penalty. With a scholarship, penalty is assessed on the amount withdrawn in excess of the scholarship award. Earnings portion of any withdrawal is subject to federal income tax liabilities.	May be rolled over, tax/penalty-free once in any 12-month period to another State Qualified Plan	A taxpayer may claim a Hope or Lifetime-Learning and receive a qualified distribution from a 529 in the same year as long as they are not claimed for the same expenses. (Note: Can choose to waive the tax-free treatment.)
Earnings taxed at owner's rate to the recipient and 10% penalty on earnings.	Not subject to non-qualified withdrawal penalty. With a scholarship, penalty is assessed on the amount withdrawn in excess of the scholarship award. Earnings portion of any withdrawal is subject to federal income tax liabilities.	Prior to current beneficiary reaching age 30, account may be rolled over to another family member tax/penalty-free. Must be completed within 60 days.	A taxpayer may claim a Hope or Lifetime-Learning and receive a qualified distribution from a 529 in the same year as long as they are not claimed for the same expenses. (Note: Can choose to waive the tax-free treatment.)

and private schools for the 2000-2001 school year was $9,174 and $23,271, respectively. College costs have risen approximately 5% over the previous five years, roughly 2% over the long-term rate of inflation. Assuming 5% to be the future rate of growth of college costs would mean that annual average college costs in a public and private school for a newborn in 2002 at age 18, or 2020, would be $22,078 and $56,004, respectively. In 2020, the four-year costs would be nearly $90,000 for a public school and approximately $225,000 for a private school.

Both the education IRA and the 529 Plan are excellent ways to use the discipline of saving and the power of compound interest to fund educational expenses. Of course, parents and grandparents can consider contributions to a Coverdell Education IRA for your child or grandchild and to another account from which the funds can be transferred to a Roth IRA when the child or grandchild has sufficient earned income. This combined strategy addresses the cost of higher education, retirement, and other future needs.

XIII

WHEN DO I ENJOY IT?

WHAT AM I SAVING FOR?

IN the previous chapters we have analyzed how best to save, grow, and compound money. Additionally, we have shown how, given time and proper investing, modest savings and investments can grow substantially to well over $1,000,000. The obvious question is: "When do I spend any of this?" A corollary to that is: "Should I save for saving's sake?" These are very good questions.

Let me answer the second question first. There is some benefit to saving for saving's sake for several reasons. Savings and accumulated wealth are a type of insurance policy for future needs. Who knows what tomorrow will bring that may require money? Funds may be needed for an illness; they may be needed for a business opportunity; they may be needed for the down payment or purchase of a major asset; or they could be needed to provide help for a family member. Whatever the reason, that money serves as insurance to provide flexibility for possibilities not otherwise available.

There are numerous examples of people who have had good ideas to start or purchase a business but didn't have a sufficient amount of their own capital (money saved) to get the necessary loan to make the idea work. Banks typically require 20% or more of the necessary funds to be provided by the borrower.

For example, let's assume an individual has an excellent opportunity to buy a business costing $500,000 that can produce significant income. If the individual cannot produce a sufficient minimum amount of his or her own capital ($100,000 would be 20%), the bank usually cannot loan the money, and the opportunity may have slipped by forever.

PLANNING TO SPEND YOUR MONEY AND WHY ACCUMULATED WEALTH IS IMPORTANT

Saying all that, it does make sense to have a plan to spend your money. The purpose of this book is not to let you save so you can make your children and grandchildren rich (although as discussed in the preceding paragraph, this may provide them insurance and flexibility for an opportunity that would otherwise not be available). More important, having significant wealth can provide you and your children and grandchildren security and freedom to do what each of you prefers to do in life, not just what you have to do.

This freedom of choice could be the freedom to send your kids to the school of their choice. It could be the freedom to allow your spouse to stay home with the children while they are little. It could be the freedom to buy a house in a nice, safe neighborhood with good schools, or it could be the freedom to buy or start your own business. These are all examples of important choices you can make given the security and freedom of financial well-being.

The idea here is to save, invest, and compound modest sums that can become larger sums, given time. At that point, you can use some or all of the interest income and still have the principal continue to grow. You can, in effect, have your cake and eat it, too. The money you worked hard to save and grow can now work hard for you. The "when" is for you to decide, but the longer and larger you allow it to grow, the harder it can work for you when you do use it.

WAYS TO SPEND ACCUMULATED FUNDS

Let's look at an example. We discussed in Chapter 9 the consequences of spending more than necessary for depreciable large purchases. To expand on that, let's say Joe, age 20, saves $10,000 that he could have spent on a new car. Joe made a conscious choice to defer the enjoyment of the nicer car for something more practical. He invests the money in a stock fund that compounds at 12%. At age 56, the $10,000 is worth $640,000. At that time, Joe makes the decision to take next year's growth to buy a very nice new car: $640,000 x 12% = $78,800 (remember, cars are more expensive 36 years in the future). Or maybe he uses one year's interest to pay his children's college tuition or to make a substantial down payment on a new home. Using the growth for several years may allow him to do all of this over several years without invading the principal. That is an example of money working hard for you. It is about deferring instant gratification for something much better down the road.

BEGINNING BALANCE $1,000,000			
YEAR	Spendable Funds	GROWTH	END-OF-YEAR BALANCE
1	$60,000	$60,000	$1,060,000
2	$63,600	$63,600	$1,123,600
3	$67,416	$67,416	$1,191,016
4	$71,460	$71,460	$1,262,477
5	$75,748	$75,748	$1,338,225
6	$80,293	$80,293	$1,418,519
7	$85,111	$85,111	$1,503,630
8	$90,217	$90,217	$1,593,848
9	$95,630	$95,630	$1,689,479
10	$101,368	$101,368	$1,790,847
11	$107,450	$107,450	$1,898,297
12	$113,897	$113,897	$2,012,195
13	$120,731	$120,731	$2,132,926

CHART 13.1

Consider one of the plans we have discussed to save $1,000,000 and then decide what you would like to do at that time. One possibility might be to withdraw one-half of the expected annual return and let the other one-half of the expected return continue to compound. If we assume 12% average growth, you could potentially pull out 6% and still have your principal compound at a 6% rate (see Chart

13.1).[22] This chart shows the balance still growing at 6% in the far right column. In the column marked Spendable Funds, it also shows the amount, 6% of the interest, which would be available to spend each year. Using The Rule of 72, the $1,000,000 doubles in value at a 6% rate in 12 years, and likewise the income doubles from $60,000 to $120,000 in the same period (start of 13th year).

Remember, if you are drawing from a Roth IRA and are under 59½, there is income tax on the interest withdrawn and a 10% tax penalty on the withdrawal unless it meets qualifying reasons for withdrawal. If you have saved and invested $2,000 into an index fund that was not tax sheltered, and therefore taxable, you may have had low tax effects because of very few sales of stock within the fund. Possibly you could have paid those taxes out of your own yearly earnings, thereby preserving the growth even though it was in a taxable account. In that case, you would pay a lower capital gains tax rate on withdrawals.

Remember, 12% is an average return, so you could select a number of alternatives. Some could be more conservative and some more aggressive. You could put the funds into safe fixed income alternatives like CDs or treasury bills and take all or part of the interest out. In that case, you would have eliminated volatility but would also probably lower withdrawal amounts and future growth. One alternative is to take out the interest income plus some of the principal to exhaust the principal over your life expectancy or beyond.

---

[22] This chart does not reduce the compounded amount by potential income taxes.

This increases the amount that can be withdrawn because you are taking out of the principal. I am not particularly fond of this option because you may live longer than you ever expected. You might have an unexplained need in the future, and you will eliminate the ability to pass these funds on to heirs if you do exhaust the principal over time, but this is just my personal preference. In the example used in Chart 13.1, your funds provide you an income as though they are holding a job for you and still growing at the same time. The possibilities are unlimited, and the options expand the longer and larger you allow your funds to grow. Spend from part of the annual growth or income for your priorities when you need to do so, but again, the longer you can wait, the better.

XIV

WHAT CAN GO WRONG?

Where's My Guarantee?

A STUDENT athlete I coached on our local high school tennis team bought my book, read it, and then had these questions for me: "Ed, will you guarantee this return? Will you guarantee that if I put $2,000 into a Roth IRA that it will be worth $1 million in 54.8 years?" Although I feel very comfortable that these concepts are reasonable and expect them to work as described, I obviously can't guarantee the future. No one can with absolute certainty.

That, of course, would be my answer. Since I knew this student well, I jokingly told him, "In 54.8 years, I will be 114 years old—so if it doesn't work out exactly as described, come see me then and I will make it right." I am much more confident this program will work than I am that I will be around to answer the question at age 114, but I hope I get the chance to answer his question and see for sure how it works out.

Let's examine circumstances that could affect our projections. We have shown that the return of stocks has been approximately 12% over the last 75 years. No one can predict the future, but it seems reasonable to expect that historic returns are an indication of what to expect in the future. History tends to repeat itself.

Realizing that historic returns are our best indication of the future, let's see what effect lower returns would have on your accumulated savings and/or what amounts you would have to save to counteract a lower compound return.

For our example, let's use two alternate compound growth rates: 10%, which is conservative, and 8%, which should be very, very conservative. Remember, too, that even if the compound rate of return of the stock market is 12% or more in the future, if you select a fund that performs lower than average and/or that has high transaction costs, your net return could still be lower than 12%, as discussed in Chapter 8.

We can calculate how The Rule of 72 works with 10% and 8%, as well as with 12%. A 12% rate doubles every 6 years, a 10% rate every 7.2 years, and an 8% rate every 9 years.

Year	8%	Year	10%	Year	12%
0	$2,000	0.0	$2,000	0.0	$2,000
9	$4,000	7.2	$4,000	6.0	$4,000
18	$8,000	14.4	$8,000	12.0	$8,000
27	$16,000	21.6	$16,000	18.0	$16,000
36	$32,000	28.8	$32,000	24.0	$32,000
45	$64,000	36.0	$64,000	30.0	$64,000
54	$128,000	43.2	$128,000	36.0	$128,000
63	$256,000	50.4	$256,000	42.0	$256,000
72	$512,000	57.6	$512,000	48.0	$512,000
81	$1,024,000	64.8	$1,024,000	54.0	$1,024,000
		72.0	$2,048,000	60.0	$2,048,000
		79.2	$4,096,000	66.0	$4,096,000
				72.0	$8,192,000
				78.0	$16,384,000

CHART 14.1

As you can see from Chart 14.1, whereas at 12% $2,000 grows to over $1 million dollars in 54 years using The Rule of 72, it takes 64.8 years at 10% and 81 years at 8%. Additionally, while the 12% rate grows to $1,024,000 in 54 years, the 10% grows to only $512,000 in 57.6 years, and the 8% rate compounds to only $128,000 in 54 years— again showing why the rate of return is so important.

Since we know that $2,000 compounds to $1 million using a 12% rate, what amount saved once would it take to accumulate to $1 million in 54 years, using a 10% and an 8% compound rate? Using The Rule of 72, you can find out on Chart 14.2.

YEAR	8%	YEAR	10%	YEAR	12%
0	$16,000	0	$4,000	0	$2,000
9	$32,000	7.2	$8,000	6.0	$4,000
18	$64,000	14.4	$16,000	12.0	$8,000
27	$128,000	21.6	$32,000	18.0	$16,000
36	$256,000	28.8	$64,000	24.0	$32,000
45	$512,000	36.0	$128,000	30.0	$64,000
54	$1,024,000	43.2	$256,000	36.0	$128,000
		50.4	$512,000	42.0	$256,000
		57.6	$1,024,000	48.0	$512,000
				54.0	$1,024,000

CHART 14.2

From the chart, you can see that it would take $16,000 growing at an 8% compounded rate to reach over $1 million in 54 years, while $4,000 compounding at 10% could grow to over $1 million in 57.6 years. To reach $1 million exactly in 54 years, it would take $5,818 compounded at 10%.

This exercise underscores the importance of saving regularly with disciplined saving. Given reasonable time frames for growth, your goals can be reached, even if historic rates of return for stock decrease. If you save more and rates do equal 12% or more, you will be that much better off.

Sometimes in seminars that I give, students ask if $1 million will be worth much in 54 years. That is a very good question and one that can also be answered using The Rule of 72. Over the last 75-plus years, inflation has averaged 3%. Inflation, or rising prices, means that it takes more money to buy the same goods and services. Inflation works like compound interest somewhat in reverse, in that it erodes the value of money. We can figure that erosion using The Rule of 72: 72 ÷ 3% (rate of inflation) = 24 years for the value of money to be cut in half. Although I won't bore you with the calculation, in over 54 years the value of money would be cut in half a fraction over 2 times so that the buying power of $1 million would be about 1/5 of what it is today, or roughly $200,000. I hope this answer doesn't discourage anyone from saving. Remember, $200,000 in inflation-adjusted value is 100 times what $2,000 is today! Alternatively, to get $1 million in inflation-adjusted spending power, save $10,000, have it grow to $5 million in 54.8 years, and you will have $1 million in today's real spending power.

"If the bridge is out in St. Louis, we can take another route.
It may take longer, but we'll still get there."

XV

I DON'T HAVE $2000!

ONCE AGAIN, IT IS NOT THE AMOUNT;
IT IS THE DISCIPLINE AND THE REGULARITY

ONE of my main premises for students and young adults, as mentioned in an earlier chapter, is that it is not the amount that is important, it is the discipline and the regularity. So if $2,000 seems like an unreachable amount, let's look at how you can save regularly with much smaller amounts and still accumulate large sums of money—even $1,000,000.

Let's say a person saves only a dime (that's right, 10 cents) every day. The chart that follows shows how it would grow using a 12% interest and more conservative rates of 10% and 8%. In 71.5 years, it would grow to $1,000,000 at 12%. If a parent started saving for a child at birth and the parent or the child continued saving throughout the child's life, it would be worth the same at age 71 as if a 17-year-old saved $2,000 one time. (Both assume a

12% growth in a tax shelter like a Roth IRA. For the new-born, the tax shelter would occur when the child had earned income at age 15, or shortly thereafter when the child was able to have earned income and the funds were transferred to a Roth IRA at that time.)

SAVE $.10 PER DAY FOR 365 DAYS = $36.50			
YEAR	**12%**	**10%**	**8%**
1	$36	$36	$36
5	$228	$219	$211
10	$631	$579	$521
15	$1,342	$1,143	$977
20	$2,593	$2,061	$1,647
25	$4,800	$3,540	$2,631
30	$8,687	$5,921	$4,078
35	$15,539	$9,756	$6,203
40	$27,615	$15,933	$9,326
45	$48,896	$25,880	$13,914
50	$86,400	$41,900	$20,655
55	$152,496	$67,701	$30,561
60	$268,929	$109,253	$45,115
65	$474,261	$176,173	$66,500
70	$836,039	$283,948	$97,922
71.5	$1,000,000	$327,644	$109,960

CHART 15.1

If you work at it, you can find a dime a day around the house or on the street. The following charts show saving a quarter a day and a dollar a day.

Save $.25 per day for 365 days = $91.25			
Year	**12%**	**10%**	**8%**
1	$91.25	$91.25	$91.25
5	$570.00	$547.50	$527.50
10	$1,577.50	$1,447.50	$1,302.50
15	$3,355.00	$2,857.50	$2,442.50
20	$6,482.50	$5,152.50	$4,117.50
25	$12,000.00	$8,850.00	$6,577.50
30	$21,717.50	$14,802.50	$10,195.00
35	$38,847.50	$24,390.00	$15,507.50
40	$69,037.50	$39,832.50	$23,315.00
45	$122,240.00	$64,700.00	$34,785.00
50	$216,000.00	$104,750.00	$51,637.50
55	$381,240.00	$169,252.50	$76,402.50
60	$672,322.50	$273,132.50	$112,787.50
65	$1,185,652.50	$440,432.50	$166,250.00
70	$2,090,097.50	$709,870.00	$244,805.00
71.5	$2,500,000.00	$819,110.00	$274,900.00

Chart 15.2

Save $1.00 per day for 365 days = $365.00			
Year	**12%**	**10%**	**8%**
1	$365	$365	$365
5	$2,280	$2,190	$2,110
10	$6,310	$5,790	$5,210
15	$13,420	$11,430	$9,770
20	$25,930	$20,610	$16,470
25	$48,000	$35,400	$26,310
30	$86,870	$59,210	$40,780
35	$155,390	$97,560	$62,030
40	$276,150	$159,330	$93,260
45	$488,960	$258,800	$139,140
50	$864,000	$419,000	$206,550
55	$1,524,960	$677,010	$305,610
60	$2,689,290	$1,092,530	$451,150
65	$4,742,610	$1,761,730	$665,000
70	$8,360,390	$2,839,480	$979,220
71.5	$10,000,000	$3,276,440	$1,099,600

Chart 15.3

REMEMBER THE TORTOISE AND THE HARE

A dollar a day saved and invested every day is better than $2,000 saved once, in that after 55 years, you would have accumulated $1,524,960.

Where do you get a dollar a day? For some, it may come out of pocket change. For others, it may be saved out of a weekly paycheck ($7.00 per week), a bimonthly paycheck ($14–$15 per pay period), or monthly paycheck ($30 per month). However you do it, have a goal and a plan and write it down. This will help make sure you follow and stick with it.

As we discussed in budgeting, one way to increase savings is to budget your expenses, prioritizing them into essentials and nonessentials or discretionary expenses, and then cut out a few discretionary expenses to provide this amount to save. In my case, if I would cut out buying a large cherry Dr Pepper with crushed ice after work each day, and I would save $1.50 per day. That is one expense I probably won't give up, but if I did I could have enough to do what I just described.

The point is that discipline and regularity are the keys. Slow and steady wins the race, just like the fable of the tortoise and the hare.

Slow and steady wins the race!

XVI

WHAT HAVE WE LEARNED?

KEY CONCEPTS

1. Understand the Power of Compound Interest and The Rule of 72

Compound interest is the most important financial concept you can ever learn. The Rule of 72 allows you to figure how quickly money can double given a specific interest rate. Just divide the rate into 72, and that gives you the number of years it will take for an investment to double given that rate of return. Then, you can continue to double the amount for the same period of years to see how compounding really adds up. This will motivate you into action. Time and the rate of return are the important factors in compound interest.

2. Begin Saving Early in Life

Let time work for you. You cannot turn the clock back, but you can begin now. If you are under 20, you have a tremendous opportunity. Remember, $2,000 saved at age 15 growing at 12% will accumulate to over $1,000,000 by age 69. If you wait until late in life, the results are much different. Saving $2,000 at age 57 at 12% will grow to only $8,000 by age 69. Give time a chance to work for you.

3. Invest in Stocks

Stock funds are the best way to invest for the long-term. A good quality stock fund can be reasonably expected to grow at 12% annually based on historical results. Stocks will go down periodically, but by investing for the long-term you can wait out the valleys. Without the higher long-term return stocks can produce, saving early is not given the full potential to work for you.

4. Stay Safe

Buy good quality, well-diversified funds. The best way to capture the return of the market safely is to own diversified funds (funds with many stocks that closely replicate the overall market). If you own a diversified fund that replicates the market, you will be emphasizing the largest and most financially secure companies, which is owning quality. A good quality fund is one with diversification and financially secure companies and one which has also had better-than-average performance.

5. Keep Costs and Expenses Low

One way to capture the market return is to buy a fund with good long-term performance that has consistently outperformed the market over time. There is no certainty a fund with good performance will continue to beat the market, but past long-term performance is a good indicator. The other way to capture the market return is to buy an index fund, which replicates the market with very low costs. Even if you buy a good quality fund with excellent long-term performance, still be conscious of keeping costs, management fees, and transaction costs lower than average—significantly lower is even better. This improves the likelihood a fund will continue to outperform over the long haul. There are good performing stock funds that also have relatively low costs. The Morningstar ratings and other services, or your broker or banker, can help you with this.

6. Budget Your Expenses

Saving is about spending less than you earn. Earning is only half of the equation. Spending is the other half. Budgeting is about prioritizing and controlling spending choices. This allows you to make saving a high-priority choice. Consider the real cost of your decision. Ten thousand dollars saved in purchases can be invested at 12%. That $10,000 invested in a stock fund growing at 12%, using The Rule of 72, could grow to $20,000 in six years, $40,000 in 12 years, $80,000 in 18 years, $160,000 in 24 years, $320,000 in 30 years, $640,000 in 36 years, and $1,280,000 in 42 years. Consider that before you make large depreciable discretionary purchases.

7. Save and Invest on a Regular Basis

It is the discipline and the regularity of saving and investing that is important, not the amount. The best way to save is to make a payment to yourself out of your paycheck. If you are paid weekly, saving $40 per week would accumulate $2,080 in a year. If you are able to save more, do it. If you are paid with a bonus annually, consider saving from that. If you are a student with a summer job, saving $700 a month for three months will be $2,100 a year. The key is regularity more than amount. Once the payment is a habit, you won't miss it or realize you ever had it. Regularity also gives you the benefit of dollar averaging. To optimize your savings plan, consider saving in three "buckets:" one bucket of saving for emergencies or contingencies; one for short or intermediate goals—a house, car, business venture, college, etc., and one for the long haul.

8. Minimize Taxes

Eliminate or defer taxes for a significant portion of your savings. Taxes can significantly reduce the compounding effect and, therefore, the long-term growth potential of your investment. In a taxable investment, a fund with low turnover (i.e., infrequent changes in stocks), or an index fund will minimize taxes by deferring the realization of gains. Therefore, stock values will continue to grow with very little tax owed. Traditional IRAs provide deductible contributions and tax-deferred growth. These are powerful tools allowing your money to grow much more significantly than it would otherwise. The Roth IRA is an ideal choice for a young person who is earning money. Although there is no deduction from taxable income for the contribution, a young person normally will have little or no taxes because earnings are so low. Most important, the Roth grows tax-free. A Roth IRA contribution of $2,000, given 54-plus years to grow tax-free in a stock fund compounding at 12%, can accumulate to more than $1,000,000. A 15-year-old who contributes $2,000 now would be age 69 when the funds grow to $1,000,000. Because there are some restrictions on withdrawals from tax-sheltered traditional IRAs or Roth IRAs, it may make sense to save in both a Roth and in a taxable account to provide some savings that are more flexible in case of financial need. As a corollary to this tax shelter idea, take full advantage of company-sponsored pension, profit sharing, and 401(k)s that provide tax-deferred contributions and tax-deferred growth. This should be a significant factor in job choices. In effect, your employer can also do for you what you are doing for yourself, potentially magnifying the results. Education IRAs and 529 Plans use the same concept as the Roth for education needs.

9. Stick With the Plan

Commit to a long-term saving plan and stick with it. This plan will work only if you have the discipline not to cash it in prematurely. There will be many opportunities to take it out early, but you should avoid doing so in all except the most dire situations. Think of at least a certain portion of your saved funds as untouchable, as though they were in a trust controlled by someone else for your long-term benefit.

10. Enjoy It!

Someday your money saved and accumulated will work for you. It is your decision when that will take place. Ideally, you have saved and invested in several buckets, including easily accessible funds for intermediate goals and long-term savings, at least some of which is in tax shelters like the Roth IRA. When funds have accumulated sufficiently, you can consider spending all of the interest one year or half of the return every year. With $1,000,000 of accumulated wealth, one half of a 12% return would be $60,000 per year, while the other half of the return is still compounding. Importantly, $60,000 of annual expendable income is not bad on a one-time $2,000 investment. Remember, if money comes out of tax shelters, like a Roth prior to age $59\frac{1}{2}$ and other than from the principal, there will be taxes on the accumulated interest and penalties, unless withdrawals are for allowable expenses.

It really is simple. Be disciplined, save regularly and often, and sooner rather than later. Invest wisely and take advantage of favorable tax shelters. Be patient. Two thousand dollars can grow to $1,000,000. Start today, and someday you can be a millionaire.

ABOUT THE AUTHOR

ED Douglas has been in banking for more than 28 years. He is the chairman and chief executive officer of Citizens Bancshares Co., a rural banking company with nearly $1 billion in assets and offices in 20 towns in north central Missouri. Ed is also a certified financial planner and a trust officer, and previously served as an investment officer and stock fund manager for Citizens Bancshares.

Ed has been active in both state and local organizations. He was appointed to a number of statewide commissions by two different governors. He recently completed his term as vice chairman of the Missouri Department of Transportation. He is a former president of the Board of Regents of Northwest Missouri State University, his alma mater, and has served as a member of the Missouri Total Transportation Commission, the Task Force on Critical Choices for Higher Education, and the Missouri Banker's Board.

He has won awards for service including the Distinguished Service Award from Northwest Missouri State University, the Missouri Economic Development Volunteer of the Year from the Southern Industrial Development Council, and the Bill Hoyt Distinguished Service Award.

Ed is an avid tennis player, a marathon runner, and is a coach of the local high school tennis team.

Ed and his wife, Marla, have three children and live in Chillicothe, Missouri.